Christ
of the
Celts

Christ
of the
Celts

The Healing of Creation

J. Philip Newell

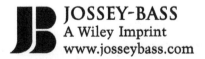

JOSSEY-BASS
A Wiley Imprint
www.josseybass.com

Published by Jossey-Bass
A Wiley Imprint
989 Market Street, San Francisco, CA 94103-1741—www.josseybass.com

All biblical quotations are from the *New Revised Standard Version Bible* (New York: Oxford University Press, 1989).

Readers should be aware that Internet Web sites offered as citations and/or sources for further information may have changed or disappeared between the time this was written and when it is read.

Jossey-Bass books and products are available through most bookstores. To contact Jossey-Bass directly call our Customer Care Department within the U.S. at 800-956-7739, outside the U.S. at 317-572-3986, or fax 317-572-4002.

Jossey-Bass also publishes its books in a variety of electronic formats. Some content that appears in print may not be available in electronic books.

Library of Congress Cataloging-in-Publication Data

Newell, J. Philip.
    Christ of the Celts : the healing of creation / J. Philip Newell.
        p. cm.
    Includes bibliographical references.
    ISBN 978-0-470-18350-2 (cloth)
        1. Spirituality—Celtic Church.   2. Creation—History of doctrines.   I. Title.
    BR748.N48 2008
    230.089'916—dc22

                                                                    2007052248

Printed in the United States of America
FIRST EDITION
HB Printing   V10010766_060519

Contents

To the Community of Casa del Sol

Blessed are those who know their need
for theirs is the grace of heaven.
Blessed are the humble
for they are close to the sacred earth.
Blessed are those who weep
for their tears will be wiped away.
Blessed are the forgiving
for they are free.
Blessed are those who hunger for earth's oneness
for they will be satisfied.
Blessed are the clear in heart
for they see the Living Presence.
Blessed are those who suffer for what is right
for theirs is the strength of heaven.
Blessed are the peacemakers
for they are born of God.

—The Casa del Sol Blessings of Jesus

Prelude

There is a longing for peace deep within the human soul today. It is a yearning within us and between us in the most important relationships of our lives. It is a yearning among us as nations and as an entire earth community. Yet ranged against this longing for peace are some of the most threatening forces that history has seen. These are forces of fear and fragmentation. And they are wedded to the mightiest political powers and religious fundamentalisms of the world today. Yet deeper still I believe is the longing for peace.

A few months ago, I gathered with over a hundred people in the high desert of New Mexico at the retreat center of Casa del Sol to pray for peace. During the chants and prayers, which ranged from longings for reconciliation in our families to cries for what we are doing to the body of the earth, there was opportunity to place a twig in the fire at the heart of the courtyard as a symbol of prayer. An eleven-year-old boy was the first to step forward, and he said clearly for us all to hear, "People often feel that children don't think about peace. But I want to be part of making peace in the world." He then cast his twig into the flame.

I do not believe that this boy's words are an exception. I believe that they come from a place deep in the human soul. It may be a place that we have become distant from. And it may be a place that has become hardened over by the pain and bitterness of life's experiences and divisions. But it is deep in the heart of our being. It does not belong exclusively to the Christian soul or the Muslim soul or the Jewish soul. It belongs to the human soul. And it is cause for great hope. But how do we serve it? How do we set it free for the healing of our lives and world?

There is widespread disillusionment within the Christian household today. And by Christian household I am not referring solely to those who attend church. I am including the much vaster number of us who have grown up in Christian families or Christian cultures and who choose to have little to do with the church. There is despair about much of what Christianity has to offer. So many of its teachings and practices seem either irrelevant to the deepest yearnings of the human soul or flatly opposed to them. Why? Is it not in part because we have been taught to distrust our deepest yearnings rather than to see them as sacred? And is it not also because we have been given the impression that Christ comes to subdue or deny our deepest desires rather than to nurture and heal them?

At key moments of transition in the history of Christianity, inspired Christian teachers have asked, "Who is Christ for us today?" That is the question that the great German pastor, Dietrich Bonhoeffer, asked in the midst of the terrible wrongs that were being done in Nazi Germany. The question, he believed, was not "Who has Christ always been?" but "Who is Christ now?" We too live at a time of transition as well as a time of deep wrong. And we are in the midst of a change of age. Never before has humanity been more aware of the oneness of the earth, even though that awareness is being opposed by some of the world's mightiest political and religious forces. The growing consciousness is that life is interwoven, that reality is a web of interrelated influences, and that what we do to a part we do to the whole. So who is Christ for us now? What is it we are to bring from the great treasure trove of our Christian household to the awarenesses and longings that are stirring within the human soul today? Can we be part of leading this new consciousness instead of opposing it or being unrelated to it?

When Christianity became the religion of the Roman Empire in the fourth century, the church moved from having a plethora of writings about Christ to a tightly defined canon of scripture that came to be known as the New Testament. The empire exerted pressure on the church to limit religious orthodoxy to what was acceptable to the state. The tragedy is that many writings were destroyed or lost. Fragments have survived, and hidden manuscripts such as *The Gospel of Thomas* have come to light to disclose to the modern world other ways of seeing Christ. Among these is *The Acts of John*, a second-century document that provides us with an image that is relevant to the new consciousness of life's unity and the longings for peace.

The Acts of John includes a description of the Last Supper. At the end of the meal, Jesus invites his disciples to form a circle, and they begin a simple Hebrew circle dance together. Jesus stands in the middle of the circle and says, "I will pipe, dance all of you! . . . I will mourn, lament all of you!"[1] His words point to the dance of life. They point also to the brokenness of the dance and to the sufferings that disharmony brings. "The whole universe takes part in the dance," he says.[2] Jesus is speaking of a harmony at the heart of life. And he is pointing to a way of moving in relation to all things, even though he knows also the price of living in relation to such a unity.

To see Christ as leading us further into the unity of life is a belief that was cherished in the ancient Celtic world. I have spoken of the new longing for peace today and the growing consciousness of the earth's oneness. But this is an ancient longing and a perennial wisdom. All the great spiritual traditions of humanity have pointed in their distinct ways to the Oneness from which we come and the Oneness that we long for. The Celtic tradition has done this through its love of Christ. He is viewed as leading us not into a separation from the world and the rest of humanity but into a renewed relationship with the Ground of Life, the One from whom all things come.

And so the Celtic tradition has some important contributions to make today. That is not to say that we all need to become Celtic Christians, which would be as absurd as saying that we all need to become Roman Catholics or Jehovah's Witnesses. These are the definitions of the past that have been used to separate us. What we need today are insights and spiritual practices that remind us of the Unity of our origins and that further nourish the longing for peace that is stirring among us. The Celtic tradition offers these to us while at the same time being deeply aware of the disharmonies within and between us that shake the very foundations of life. This is not a tradition that is naive regarding the destructive energies of evil.

I will be drawing on material that ranges from the earliest centuries after Christ through to today. Some of these sources historically have been hidden or lost sight of, such as *The Acts of John* and *The Secret Book of John*. Others, such as the biblical gospel of John, have been available all along although viewed through lenses colored by the imperial orthodoxy of the fourth century and following. The Celtic tradition cherishes the memory of the one whom Jesus especially loved. John is remembered as leaning against Jesus at the Last Supper. It was said of him that he therefore heard the Heartbeat of God.

He becomes an image of listening within life for the beat of God's presence. And so I will draw on the writings associated with John the Beloved and his community in Asia Minor over the first centuries, using both canonical and noncanonical texts and legends.

In addition to these, I shall refer to the great teachers of the Celtic world who draw heavily on John and his memory, from as early as Irenaeus in second-century Gaul through Eriugena in ninth-century Ireland to Teilhard de Chardin in twentieth-century France. These teachers have stirred reaction from Western orthodoxy over the centuries, for again and again they point to the essential harmony between Christ and creation.

In Chapter One, "The Memory of the Song," I explore the Celtic image of Christ as the memory of what we have forgotten. He remembers the dance of the universe and the harmony that is deep within all things. He is the memory also of who we are. He shows us not a foreign truth but a truth that is hidden in the depths of the human soul. He comes to wake us up, to call us back to ourselves and to the relationship that is deep within all things. The emphasis is not on becoming something other than ourselves but on becoming truly ourselves. Christ discloses to us the sacred root of our being and of all being. This has enormous implications for how we view ourselves and one another and how we approach the deepest energies within us and within all things. It invites us to change the way we move in the dance of life together as nations, as individuals, and as an entire earth community.

To speak of Christ as the memory of the harmony within all things is to question many of the teachings that have dominated Christian thought and practice over the centuries. We have neglected the truth that we and all life come from the same Source and that all things therefore carry within them the sound of the Beginning. And so in Chapter Two, "A Forgotten Tune," I explore how the doctrine of original sin, so dominant in Western Christian thought, has fed discord within us and between us rather than enabling the dance. It has given us the impression that what is deepest in the human soul is essentially opposed to God. The traditional answer has therefore been that our essence needs to be changed, which in turn puts us at odds with the rest of humanity and the rest of the created order. In the Celtic tradition, Christ comes to remind us of the tune, not a strange tune that comes from afar but a deeply familiar tune that we have forgotten. It is the tune at the heart of our being and all being.

In Chapter Three, "The Rhythm of the Earth," I look at the Celtic belief that the universe comes out of the womb of the Eternal. The Genesis story at the beginning of the Bible is pointing not to an event that occurred in the distant past. It is pointing to the ever-unfolding mystery of life in the cosmos and to the Heart from which all things come now. Matter, therefore, whether the moist matter of the fecund earth or the exploding matter of burning stars, is not a neutral substance put in motion by a distant Creator. The matter of creation is a holy and living energy born from the hidden depths of God. The universe is a single organism that carries within itself one ancient rhythm. It is a body with one Heartbeat. Christ comes to lead us back into the dance. In him we hear the beat that comes from the heart of all things.

"Empty Notes," Chapter Four, explores another traditional doctrine that impedes the dance today. It is the doctrine of creation *ex nihilo*, the belief that God created the world out of nothing. The great Celtic teachers over the centuries have said that creation does not come out of nothing. It comes out of God. The belief that matter is made from nothing is like saying that the basic notes or elements of the universe are empty, that they do not carry within themselves the sound of God's Being. This is exactly what the imperial religion of the fourth century was content to say. It allowed the Holy Roman Empire, as it has allowed Western empires ever since, to exploit matter and to dominate nations and peoples. It has made room for a subordinating of the physical and of humanity's birthing energies, including a subordination of the feminine. Instead, in the Celtic tradition, Christ comes to show us that matter matters. Creation will be saved only if we learn to revere matter, whether that be the matter of our human bodies, the matter of the body of the earth, or the matter of the body politic and how we relate to one another as sovereign nations. The elemental notes of the universe are alive with Spirit.

Christ leads us not away from matter but more deeply into the stuff of the universe and the stuff of daily life and relationship. And he discloses to us that the deepest note in the universe is love and the longing for union. So in Chapter Five, "The Sound of Love," I explore the Celtic belief that the Heartbeat of life is Love. That is the first and deepest sound within the unfolding cosmos. It vibrates at the heart of all things. Christ is viewed as disclosing the passion of God to us. The cross is a theophany or showing of Love and the desire for oneness. It reveals God rather than appeases God. So in the Celtic tradition, the cross reveals also what is deepest in us. By disclosing to us the Heart of all being, Christ discloses to us the heart of our own being. The cross reveals that we approach our true selves as we give ourselves away to one another in love. This is when we come closest to truly finding ourselves. The whole cosmos is a Self-giving of God. And we will find our place in the great dance only to the extent that we love.

"Paying the Piper," Chapter Six, is an exploration of another major disharmony in our Western Christian inheritance. It is the notion of God needing to be paid to forgive us, the cross as a type of blood sacrifice to purchase salvation for sinful humanity. Does this not fly in the face of everything we most deeply know about love? Think of the people who have truly loved us in our lives. Would they ever require payment to forgive? And yet the doctrine of substitutionary atonement, in which the death of Christ is viewed as a substitute payment for the life of our souls, has been allowed to occupy central ground in the landscape of Christian teaching and practice. We have created the impression that judgment, not love, is the deepest note in the universe, and that the Piper has to be paid to change his tune. This in turn has created the impression that division and vengeance are the deepest sounds within the human soul. It has undermined the deeper longing for peace.

Chapter Seven, "The Hymn of the Universe," explores the one song that we and all things are part of. It is a cosmic song and a personal song. It is both vast and intimate. At the heart of matter, at the heart of every atom in the cosmos, is the Eternal Presence. And it is a Presence that calls us each by name. In the Celtic world, the high-standing crosses that are rooted deep in the ancient landscape express the belief that Christ and creation are inseparably interwoven. Two images combine to make one form in the Celtic cross. Christ, represented by the cross, and creation, represented by the orb at the heart of the cross, are one. They share the same center. They come forth from the same point. Together they emerge out of the heart of God's Being. And so the deeper we move in relation to creation and the deeper we move within us and between us, the closer we come to the Personal Presence that Christ embodies. The hymn of the universe is as vast as the cosmos. It is as intimate as the closest relationship. Each of us is the partner of the Beloved in the dance.

Chapter Eight, "Broken Cadences," explores the doctrine of individual salvation as an obstacle in recovering our sense of the oneness of the universe. It gives the impression that one part can be complete when the other parts are broken. It would be like my saying that I can be well when my child is suffering or that any of us can be complete when our nation is being false to itself or that we as a human race can be healthy when the body of the earth is infected. It runs counter to everything we now know about the body of reality. Wholeness does not come in isolation. It comes in relationship to the whole. And so as we ask the question "Who is Christ for us today?" it is increasingly meaningless to answer with the traditional teaching that he is the Savior of our individual souls. In what sense can individual strands be torn from the one fabric of reality and be considered complete? My well-being will come only in relationship to our well-being and the well-being of all things. We are being invited to seek a new salvation. It will come through and with one another, not in separation from one another.

It is the ancient Wholeness of which we are a part. It is the recovery of the Hymn of the Universe, not broken cadences plucked from the whole.

The young boy who placed his twig on the growing flame is a sign of such a recovery. And his desire is a longing that is being heard deep in the human soul today. Will we in the Christian household choose to be part of kindling that desire within ourselves and within one another, or will we choose to ignore it? Will we in a spirit of humility root ourselves again in the Humus or Ground of Life from which we and all things come, or will we continue to claim that our path is essentially separate? The consequences are great. It will be a movement toward greater harmony or deeper discord.

I realized as the young boy placed his twig in the fire that evening that there were tears in many eyes, including mine. Tears can be a life-giving signal for us in our lives, both individually and collectively. They can indicate that vital places within us that have become dormant are being stirred afresh. They can also be a type of washing of the inner lens. We have come to see certain things most clearly in our lives and relationships only through tears, the tears of pain and loss or the tears of delight and laughter. I know in my own life, whether as a father weeping over the mental illness of one of my children or crying at the birth of that same child years ago or as a son of the earth despairing at what we are doing to one another as nations or crying at the beauty of sunrise over a war-torn Middle Eastern desert, that tears are part of being more fully alive. To pay attention to our tears is to hear the deepest longings of the human soul. It is to hear again the ancient yearning for well-being and harmony.

CHAPTER 1

The Memory of the Song

I was in San Jose in the summer of 2006. When I am on the road teaching, I like to have an afternoon siesta to replenish my strength. Sometimes I enter quite a deep sleep, and as I wake, it is as if I am climbing out of a place deep in the unconscious. The climb is gradual, and it takes me awhile to reach the surface of wakefulness again. As I began to resurface that afternoon in San Jose, I was aware of the sound of music. It was coming from the garden courtyard just outside my room. A table was being prepared for an evening meal with invited guests. So the music was intermingled with the gentle clinking sounds of wineglasses and silverware being laid. But in my half-wakeful state, the music was not a recording. It was a live ensemble of strings and pipes playing a song that came from a distant place. And the meal was a banquet in an ancient garden courtyard to which we all were invited. I lay for a long time drifting between sleep and consciousness, allowing myself to remember.

What is it we have forgotten about ourselves and one another? In the Celtic tradition, the Garden of Eden is not a place in space and time from which we are separated. It is the deepest dimension of our being from which we live in a type of exile. It is our place of origin or genesis in God. Eden is home, but we live far removed from it. And yet in the Genesis account, the Garden is not destroyed. Rather Adam and Eve become fugitives from the place of their deepest identity. It is a picture of humanity living in exile.

At the beginning of the Hebrew scriptures, the Book of Genesis describes humanity as made in the "image" and "likeness" of God (Genesis 1:26). This is a fundamental truth in our biblical inheritance. Everything else that is said about us in the scriptures needs to be read in the light of this starting point. The image of God is at the core of our being. And like the Garden, it has not been destroyed. It may have become covered over or lost sight of, but it is at the beginning of who we are.

A nineteenth-century teacher in the Celtic world, Alexander Scott, used the analogy of royal garments. Apparently in his day, royal garments were woven through with a costly thread, a thread of gold. And if somehow the golden thread were taken out of the garment, the whole garment would unravel. So it is, he said, with the image of God woven into the fabric of our being. If it were taken out of us, we would unravel. We would cease to be. So the image of God is not simply a characteristic of who we are, which may or may not be there, depending on whether or not we have been baptized. The image of God is the essence of our being. It is the core of the human soul. We are sacred not because we have been baptized or because we belong to one faith tradition over another. We are sacred because we have been born.

But what does it mean to be made in the image of God? What does it mean to say that the Garden is our place of deepest identity? In part, it is to say that wisdom is deep within us, deeper than the ignorance of what we have done or become. It is to say that the passion of God for what is just and right is deep within, deeper than any apathy or participation in wrong that has crippled us. To be made in the image of God is to say that creativity is at the core of our being, deeper than any barrenness that has dominated our lives and relationships. And above all else, it is to say that love and the desire to give ourselves away to one another in love is at the heart of who we are, deeper than any fear or hatred that holds us hostage. Deep within us is a longing for union, for our genesis is in the One from whom all things have come. Our home is the Garden, and deep within us is the yearning to hear its song again.

In *The Secret Book of John*, a second-century manuscript recovered at Nag Hammadi, Egypt, in 1945 along with *The Gospel of Thomas* and other lost accounts of Jesus, John the Beloved has a dreamlike encounter with Christ. John has been weeping in grief and uncertainty after the events of the crucifixion. But through his tears, he becomes aware of Christ's presence. This is a favorite theme in John's writings, seeing through tears. We know that pain and loss in our lives can make us close down to life or harden us with bitterness. But John explores the way in which tears can open us up to see what we have not noticed before. It is as if the inner lens of our heart is washed and we see what previously was clouded from sight. What are the tears in our lives today, individually and collectively, the losses within our families and the grief within the human soul at what we are doing to one another as nations and religious communities? John's experience invites us not to shut down to these tears but to see through them and to be opened to what we have not known before or have long ago forgotten.

Christ says to John, in this brief account, that humanity has forgotten itself. We suffer from a "bond of forgetfulness," he says.[1] We do not know ourselves, nor do we remember our beginnings. We are in what is like a deep sleep. And the more distant we become from our true self, the more we fall under the sway of the false self, or what he calls "the counterfeit spirit."[2] There are three major symptoms to this "bond of forgetfulness," he says. They are ignorance, falseness, and above all, anxiety. When we lose touch with the wisdom that is within us, we live out of ignorance. When we no longer remember the truth of who we are, we become slaves to falseness. And when we forget the deep root of our being, we become prone to fear and anxiety.

My eldest son, Brendan, suffered a psychotic breakdown in the summer of 2000 when he was sixteen years old. I was overwhelmed as a father—and again and again at times over these years have been overwhelmed—by a sense of not knowing what to do to help him. And Brendan, of course, is not alone. There are countless young men and women in our world today who are manifesting the deep fears and anxieties of our age. Fear is not only in them; it is in us. It is part of the human psyche. And it is multiplying rapidly. What are we to do to help? How do we enable them and ourselves to hear again the song of our beginnings and to recover the harmony that is within us and between us?

When Brendan became well enough to leave Edinburgh, I took him to the Cairngorm mountains in the highlands of Scotland for a few days of hiking. It is a place of cherished memory for us as a family, of hiking and vacationing together. It is also a place where one can walk for hours without meeting others. I thought it would feel like a safe place for my son in the midst of his often paralyzing fears. The first day, we walked for hours through Glen Feshie without meeting another soul. It seemed that we had made the right decision. But around midday, turning out of the glen to head up Sgoran Dubh, a favorite mountain peak, we noticed two men working on the path ahead of us with pickaxes and shovels. In Brendan's mind, they were there to do him harm, so we needed to give wide berth to get around them. No sooner had we passed, however, than Brendan began to worry about the return journey. They would be there waiting for us.

On the way back, it took all my powers of persuasion to keep Brendan on the single path that leads up and down that mountain. On the far side of Sgoran Dubh is a sheer drop into Gleann Einich. But Brendan kept trying to persuade me to scramble over the steep edge rather than return to the point where we had met the workmen earlier in the day. It was a painful experience for me as a father to feel the dementing effects of fear in my son. By the time we returned to the glen, the workmen were gone. But I was shaken by having witnessed the close relationship between fear and truly mad behavior. We know this relationship in our lives and world today. We experience it within ourselves, and we witness it on an international scale as we are driven as nations toward the precipitous edge of truly destructive policies and actions.

Christ says to John that he is our memory. Humanity has forgotten itself. It has become subject to fears and falseness and ignorance. "I am the memory of the fullness," says Christ.[3] He comes to wake us up, both to ourselves and to one another. He carries within himself the true memory of our nature and of the fullness of our relationship with all things. He comes to release us from the falseness of what we are doing to one another. These themes from *The Secret Book of John* are similar to what we hear in the gospel of John. Jesus says that he has come "that those who do not see may see" (John 9:39). Or as he asserts in his trial before the Roman governor, "For this I was born, and for this I came into the world, to testify to the truth" (John 18:37). He is the memory of the song. He witnesses to the truth of who we are.

I do not believe that the *gospel*, which literally means "good news," is given to tell us that we have failed or been false. That is not news, and it is not good. We already know much of that about ourselves. We know we have been false, even to those whom we most love in our lives and would most want to be true to. We know we have failed people and whole nations throughout the world today, who are suffering or who are subjected to terrible injustices that we could do more to prevent. So the gospel is not given to tell us what we already know. Rather, the gospel is given to tell us what we do not know or what we have forgotten, and that is who we are, sons and daughters of the One from whom all things come. It is when we begin to remember who we are, and who all people truly are, that we will begin to remember also what we should be doing and how we should be relating to one another as individuals and as nations and as an entire earth community.

One of the greatest teachers in the Celtic world, John Scotus Eriugena in ninth-century Ireland, also taught that Christ is our memory. We suffer from the "soul's forgetfulness," he says.[4] Christ comes to reawaken us to our true nature. He is our epiphany. He comes to show us the face of God. He comes to show us also our face, the true face of the human soul. This leads the Celtic tradition to celebrate the relationship between nature and grace. Instead of grace being viewed as opposed to our essential nature or as somehow saving us from ourselves, nature and grace are viewed as flowing together from God. They are both sacred gifts. The gift of nature, says Eriugena, is the gift of "being"; the gift of grace, on the other hand, is the gift of "well-being."[5] Grace is given to reconnect us to our true nature. At the heart of our being is the image of God, and thus the wisdom of God, the creativity of God, the passions of God, the longings of God. Grace is opposed not to what is deepest in us but to what is false in us. It is given to restore us to the core of our being and to free us from the unnaturalness of what we are doing to one another and to the earth.

As a father, when I witnessed the paralyzing fears of my son in Glen Feshie, I did not confuse Brendan's illness with his deepest identity. I did not assume that that was his true nature. In fact, part of what I remembered during that agonizing experience was how he had run wild and free as a boy in that same glen, how he had uninhibitedly dabbled his feet in the flowing waters of the Feshie, how he had tumbled carefree in the thick heather. In other words, I remembered Brendan. And I longed for the day, as I long every day in prayer, for the healing graces that will free him and our world from the fears that separate us from the deepest song of our being.

Christ is often referred to in the Celtic tradition as the truly natural one. He comes not to make us more than natural or somehow other than natural but to make us truly natural. He comes to restore us to the original root of our being. As the twentieth-century French mystic-scientist Teilhard de Chardin says much later in the Celtic world, grace is "the seed of resurrection" sown in our nature.[6] It is given not to make us something other than ourselves but to make us radically ourselves. Grace is given not to implant in us a foreign wisdom but to make us alive to the wisdom that was born with us in our mother's womb. Grace is given not to lead us into another identity but to reconnect us to the beauty of our deepest identity. And grace is given not that we might find some exterior source of strength but that we might be established again in the deep inner security of our being and in learning to lose ourselves in love for one another to truly find ourselves.

This is not to pretend that there are not infections deep within us and deep within the interrelationships of life. Eriugena refers to sin as an infection, "leprosy of the soul."[7] And just as leprosy distorts the human face and makes it appear grotesque and ugly, so sin distorts the countenance of the soul and makes it appear monstrous, so much so that we come to believe that that is the face of the human soul. And just as leprosy is a disease of insensitivity, of loss of feeling, so sin leads us into an insensitivity to what is deepest within us, and more and more we treat one another as if we were not made in the image of God. Eriugena makes the point that in the gospel story when Jesus heals the lepers, he does not give them new faces. Rather he restores them to their true faces and to the freshness of their original countenances. Grace reconnects us to what is first and deepest in us. It restores us to the root of our well-being, which is deeper than the infections that threaten our minds and souls and relationships.

Alexander Scott, the nineteenth-century Celtic teacher, uses the analogy of a plant suffering from blight. If such a plant were shown to botanists, even if the botanists had never seen that type of plant before, they would define it in terms of its essential life features. They would identify the plant with reference to its healthy properties of height and color and scent. They would not define it in terms of its blight. Rather they would say that the blight is foreign to the plant, that it is attacking the essence of the plant. Now this may seem a very obvious point botanically. But maybe it is so obvious that we have missed the point when it comes to defining human nature. We have tended to define ourselves and one another in terms of the blight, in terms of sin or evil, in terms of the failings or illnesses of our lives, instead of seeing what is deeper still, the beauty of the image of God at the core of our being.

When Eriugena and other Celtic teachers speak of Christ as our memory, as the one who leads us to our deepest identity, as the one who remembers the song of our beginnings, they are not ignoring the depth of sin's infection. They are not suggesting that our true self is just under the surface of a film of falseness, easily recovered, or that the harmony deep within all things can be recaptured with just a bit of fine tuning. The infections within the human soul are chronic. There are diseases of greed and limited self-interest among us as individuals and as nations that are ageless, so much so that we can hardly imagine what the true harmony of the earth sounds like. These are not just superficial infections. They are tangled in the very roots of our being. They are cancerous. And some of them need to be surgically removed.

Eriugena uses the analogy of sin pouncing on everything that is born. In commenting on the words from Genesis 4, "Sin is lurking at the door, its desire is for you," Eriugena says that sin is hovering at the door of the womb, ready to infect everything that comes into being.

Given what we now know of the interrelatedness of life and how even the unborn child is infected by the psychological scars of its family or by the pollution of its wider environment, we may wish to say that sin is lurking inside the door of the womb. The shadow comes very close to the beginning of our lives, but deeper still is the Light from which we come. The conception of all life in the universe is sacred.

To say that the root of every person and creature is in God, rather than opposed to God, has enormous implications for how we view ourselves, including our deepest physical, sexual, and emotional energies. It also profoundly affects the way we view one another, even in the midst of terrible failings and falseness in our lives and world. Satan is sometimes referred to by Eriugena and other Celtic teachers as Angel of Light. This is a way of pointing to the deepest identity of everything that has being, whether creaturely or angelic. The extent to which our energies, and the energies of any created thing, are evil and destructive is the extent to which we are not being truly ourselves.

Eriugena may well have believed literally in a personal presence and source of evil, named Satan, as did most of the medieval world, whether Celtic or imperial. More significantly, however, he is inviting us to be aware of our own capacity for falseness and the potential for distortion in everything that has been created. But most important of all, he is recalling us to our deepest identity as born of Light. We become sinful to the extent that we are not being truly ourselves. We become false to the extent that we are not living from the true root of our being. And Eriugena is pointing also to the path of healing and transformation. We find new beginnings not by looking away from the conflicting energies that stir within us but by looking within them for the sacred Origin of life and desire. In the midst of confusions and struggle in our lives, we are being invited to search deeper than the shadows for the Light of our beginnings. It is also the Light of our true end.

A number of years ago, I delivered a talk in Ottawa, Canada, on some of these themes. I referred especially to the prologue of the gospel of John and his words concerning "the true light that enlightens everyone coming into the world" (John 1:9). I was inviting us to watch for that Light within ourselves, in the whole of our being, and to expect to glimpse that Light at the heart of one another and deep within the wisdom of other traditions. At the end of the talk, a Mohawk elder, who had been invited to comment on the common ground between Celtic spirituality and the native spirituality of his people, stood with tears in his eyes. He said, "As I have listened to these themes, I have been wondering where I would be today. I have been wondering where my people would be today. And I have been wondering where we would be as a Western world today if the mission that came to us from Europe centuries ago had come expecting to find Light in us."

We cannot undo the terrible wrongs that have been done in our collective history and in the name of Christ. We can, however, be part of a new birthing within us and between us today. And the new birthing relates to the ancient song that we are invited to hear again. It may seem such a distant song that we hear it only as in a dream. But the more we become reacquainted with its music, the more we will come to know that the deepest notes within us and between us in our world are not discord. They form an ancient harmony.

CHAPTER 2

A Forgotten Tune

I have been writing this book in the early hours of the morning. And here on the holy island of Lindisfarne, where I am leading a retreat, and which since the seventh century has been a vital place of Celtic art and learning, I woke early and was aware of a dream that had been with me through the night. I dreamt that my second daughter, Kirsten, was being told she was a fool. Repeatedly, she was being subjected to the impression that she was stupid, that she knew nothing. And I saw the look on her face. She was hurt. At one level, she knew that this was not right. But at another level, the description was sowing uncertainty in her, and she became increasingly unable to express herself coherently, so plagued was she by doubt. The dream relates directly to the theme of this chapter. It relates also to the fact that for dessert last night, we were served raspberry fool! The unconscious points, sometimes comically, to the interrelatedness of life.

What I saw in my dream is the tragedy that we witness again and again in life. If a child grows up being told she is ugly or stupid or selfish, at some level, she comes to believe that about herself. The descriptions haunt her self-understanding, and she lives in a state of doubt about her deepest identity. This is exactly what has happened in relation to the doctrine of original sin, a belief that has dominated the landscape of Western Christian thought and practice since the fourth century. It teaches that what is deepest in us is opposed to God rather than of God. It means that we are essentially ignorant rather than bearers of light, that we are essentially ugly rather than rooted in divine beauty, that we are essentially selfish rather than made in the image of love—the list goes on and on. It is a doctrine that disempowers us. It feeds our forgetfulness of the sacred tune at the heart of our being. And its corollary is the belief that Christ embodies a song that is essentially foreign to us. The consequences, both individually and collectively, have been disastrous.

One of the earliest Christian writers in the Celtic world, Pelagius from Wales, foresaw the consequences in the fourth century. It led him to oppose the doctrine of original sin with all his might. His concern was that if the Church defined the human soul as essentially sinful, it would undermine us in our journey toward wholeness. It would pervert how we viewed ourselves and our deepest energies. It would distance Christ from what is at the core of our being. And it would distort the way we approached the people and teachings of other traditions. He was right to be passionate. It is a doctrine that has wreaked untold havoc in the lives and relationships of countless men and women in the Western world, including the self-perceptions of generation after generation of children. It has distanced Christ from the heart of the human soul. And it continues to undermine the way we relate, or choose not to relate, to the people and wisdoms of other cultures and communities.

Pelagius, who had become a well-known Christian teacher in Rome and then in Palestine, was banned from the Roman Empire in the year 418 on a charge of disturbing the peace. Several months later, he was excommunicated from the imperial church on a charge of heresy. There are many strands to this story, but one of them relates to power and its abuse. The doctrine of original sin was a convenient "truth" for the builders of empire. They could continue to conquer the world and subdue peoples. And now they could do it with the authority of a divine calling. What the world needed and what the masses throughout the empire required was the truth that they, with their ecclesiastical princes, possessed. Truth was to be distributed from above. It was to be a religion of dependency. And part of the conflict with Pelagius and other teachers in the Celtic mission was that a people who believed they were made in the image of God and were therefore bearers of an ancient wisdom and an unspeakable dignity were not a people that could be easily cowed by power and external authority. The empire and its church chose to neglect the sacred tune at the heart of the human soul. Instead they heard only a profane disharmony that had to be denounced and dominated.

To be rid of Pelagius, however, was not an easy matter. Repeated imperial councils of the church condemned him and his teachings, in ways that indicated how threatened they continued to be by his insights. In the end, the most effective method was to misrepresent him. Pelagius had taught that when we look into the face of a newborn child, we are looking into the face of God freshly born among us. Of course, he was not speaking simply of the newborn child. He was pointing to the deepest dimension of the human soul. Deep within us is the wisdom of God, the creativity of God, the longings of God. He taught that although our nature is sacred, it is deeply wounded and in need of the healing energies of grace. Christ comes to restore us to our true depths. He was represented as saying, however, that because our nature is sacred, we have no need of grace, we have no need of Christ. This misrepresentation has clung to his name over the centuries and continues to be the standard line on Pelagius in most Western Christian teaching institutions. They have also claimed that there are no writings available from his hand so that all we can know about him comes through the mouth of his theological opponents. These misrepresentations continue, even among the most respected of theologians, despite the fact that manuscripts like his *Letter to Demetrias* clearly state that Christ comes with grace to reconnect us to our nature.

Which one of us is prepared to say with the historical church that the newborn child we hold in our arms is essentially sinful? I am not prepared to say this about my four children or about anyone's children. And in my travels, I meet countless numbers of men and women, mothers and fathers of children throughout the Western world, who similarly reject this definition. In Lynchburg, Virginia, at the end of a talk in which I was exploring the beliefs of Celtic spirituality with reference to my book *Listening for the Heartbeat of God,* a woman in her eighties walked purposefully up the central aisle toward me with a copy of the book in hand. She said, "I don't normally write in books that I read, but I want to show you what I've written in this book of yours after reading it." She opened the front cover, and inside she had written, "I knew it! I knew it! I knew it!"

We have known the truth of what is at the heart of a newborn child. Yes, of course, even at birth, an infant carries within herself, in her body, mind, and soul, some of the infections of her family and environment. But when we hold her in our arms, we know at a deep level within ourselves that she is sacred. I count the births of my four children as the most holy moments of my life. What I see in their faces and smell in their skin is God. This again and again is the experience of families at the births and baptisms of their children. The parents whom I meet are not bringing their children for baptism because they think what is deepest in them is sin. They are bringing their infants to the community of faith because they know innately, with a gratitude that is beyond words, that their children carry within them the sounds and scents of the Beginning. So why have we tolerated the doctrine of original sin in our Christian inheritance? Why in our Church of England Book of Common Prayer have we been prepared to say at evensong, "There is no health in us"?[1] Or why in our Church of Scotland Westminster Confession of Faith, and in equivalent statements of faith throughout the Western church, have we given any room to the belief that we are "opposite to all good, and wholly inclined to all evil"?[2] It may be that many of us no longer literally use these words in prayer and confession, but they still haunt the Christian household. The distorted tune echoes within the walls of our sanctuaries and haunts the inner chambers of our lives.

We can hardly begin our religious services without first of all visiting the place of essential worthlessness. It is like an obsessive-compulsive disorder on a massive scale. If every time I entered the presence of those I most love I felt that first of all I had to go on about my failings, there would be reason to doubt my well-being. There would also be reason to doubt the very nature of the relationship. And yet that is exactly what we have been doing collectively for centuries in our religious household, and the family is unwell. This is not to say that naming wrong, confronting the shadow, and turning from falseness, both individually and collectively, is not a critically important part of our well-being. It is to say, however, that the naming of wrong within us and among us, like the confronting of the shadow and turning from falseness, will be life-giving only to the extent that we remember first the deepest tune of our being, which is of God. This is the foundation that will sustain true change.

There are certain things I have learned only very slowly in my life as a father of four children, and there are other things I am sure I have not learned at all. But with my youngest child, Cameron, I have become very sure that I will no longer tolerate religious services and teachings that give him the impression that he is essentially opposed to God. I will not have him sit through liturgies or sermons that subject him to the belief that his deepest energies come from a sinful place. Of course, he needs to learn to be wise in his life about the ways in which our energies—intellectual, emotional, and sexual—are confused and can become destructively distorted. And of course, participation in community is a key to his well-being, as it is to mine and that of every man and woman. But when I experience the church undermining my child's sense of self, I will choose to join the many members of our Christian household who no longer come to the family gatherings because they are no longer being fed in their souls and because there is much in our inheritance that is actually at odds with some of the deepest yearnings of the human soul today.

The decision no longer to tolerate the forgetting of the tune has been an important step in my life, not only for my son but for my own soul as well. For too long, there have been haunted places in my heart where doubts have been fed by the lingering sound of the distorted tune. And I have witnessed the same in far too many brothers and sisters. I remember as a boy accompanying my father on a preaching tour to Jamaica. At night, I had to stay apart from my parents at the home of a Jamaican family down a long, dark path. Walking home in the evenings along the unlit path with the father of the family felt strange to me, but it did not compare to the terrifying experience I had one night.

I was awakened in the middle of the night by an earth tremor. But I did not realize what it was. Being a good little evangelical boy, I thought Christ had come to take the saved to heaven. But being not such a good little evangelical boy, I thought Christ had come and left me behind. And I thought it was probably related to the fact that I had been kissing the girl next door in the backyard at home. So Christ had come and taken my family but left me. Not absolutely sure, however, I thought I should test my fears. So I called out to the mother of the household, "May I have a glass of water, please?" To my great relief, she responded, although I then began to wonder what she had done to have been left behind!

If we do not laugh at stories like this, we need to cry. They convey the damage that has been done in the psyche of even the youngest, most innocent minds. They communicate the false tension that we have experienced between natural desire and holy desire. And they portray Christ not only as distant from us and less loving than those who have most loved us in our lives but as leading us into a salvation that forsakes the earth and the rest of humanity. As a boy, I had so absorbed the doctrine of original sin into my self-understanding that I could imagine being left behind by the One whom we call Love. The prophecy of Isaiah says, "I will not forget you" (Isaiah 49:15). These words, addressed to the heart of the human soul, I was applying only to the few. Given the depth of love in my family, I should at least have known that my parents would never leave me behind—but I did not know.

There is the wonderful story of Saint Patrick on the Day of Judgment that comes down to us in the oral tradition of ancient Irish legend. Patrick is summoned to the One, in whose presence the sound of all living things can be heard and whose voice is like the flowing waters of every river. When the message is conveyed to Patrick, he responds by saying, "I will not come unless all my people may come with me." Again Patrick is summoned, and again he responds, "I will not come unless all my people may come with me." A third time Patrick is summoned, and a third time he declines. So finally the One seated on the throne at the heart of the universe says, "Tell Patrick to come, and he may come with all his people, but there is one thing Patrick must do." And there the story ends. We are not told what Patrick must do, but we know that whatever it is, he will do it so that all his people may come with him.

I should have known that my parents would not forsake me. I should have known that they would decline even heaven's company in order to care for their son. But I did not yet have the tools to see that Christ comes not from afar but from the very heart of the human soul. I did not yet see that at the core of the gospel is the truth that we are most deeply divine precisely when we are most deeply human. I did not yet see that my family's love for me was the love of Christ.

Last summer, I was exploring some of these themes with a group of retreatants at Casa del Sol in the high desert of New Mexico. One of the women in the group had been adopted as a child. She suddenly saw, or enabled us suddenly to see, that a dominant model in Western Christianity's understanding of salvation is that we are adopted by God rather than being originally and essentially children of God. Woody Allen, the American comedian, once said, "My only regret in life is that I'm not somebody else." This is typically funny of Woody Allen, but it is also typically tragic of the way many of us have grown up seeing ourselves. We have thought that the goal is to become something other than ourselves rather than to become truly ourselves.

One of the reasons the "adoption" model has been prominent in Western Christian thought is that Saint Paul's Letter to the Galatians has been translated as saying that we need "adoption as children" (Galatians 4:5). It is clear, however, in his analogy of children's being heirs to an inheritance they have not yet taken up that he is pointing not to a need to be adopted but to a need to adopt or come into possession of what is already ours. The Greek verb *apolambano* means "receive" or "claim," and in that sense "adopt" but not "be adopted." We are living as "minors," he says, rather than true heirs. We need to grow up into the maturity of our being. Christ comes to lead us into our inheritance, which, as Saint Paul says in his dialogue with Greek philosophers in Athens, is to know that we are "God's offspring" (Acts 17:28). This is the song at the heart of the human soul, not a foreign tune that leads us to seek admission into a family that is not ours.

This has radical implications for how we view ourselves and one another. It means in relation to our children that we will look for wisdom deep within their souls. It means for us that even in the midst of our worst failures, we will look for strength at the core of our being. It means in relation to others, even those who most threaten us, that we will look for the longing deep in their hearts for relationship and for harmony. And it means in relation to other cultures and religions that we will look for the light that completes the truths we hold most dear rather than competing with them.

In the recurring dream about my daughter Kirsten, I was angry about what was being said to her and how it made her feel. And now that I am awake, I want to retain that sense of anger. No child, no person, should be so treated, and no place should be given to such teachings in the Christian household. I realize that the dream is not simply about Kirsten in particular or even about children generally. It is also about me and about the young, impressionable part of myself that has been haunted by the false tune.

But when I awoke, I was thinking specifically about Kirsten and about her specific sense of self-identity. Her name kept running through my mind: "Kirsten Margaret Iona," I was saying to myself, "Kirsten Margaret Iona." And I came to see in a fresh way that that is who she is. She does not need to become something other than herself or anything other than what is most deeply within her. She is Kirsten, which literally means "Christ-One." She, like each of us, comes from the heart of God, as Christ does. Or as Gerard Manley Hopkins puts it in one of his poems, we are what Christ is, "immortal diamond."[3] She is Margaret, which means "pearl." She, like each of us, has a shining pricelessness to her being. And she is Iona, the sacred island in the sea to which pilgrims journey for healing. She, like each of us, carries within herself the sacred energies of the divine for the transformation and well-being of the world. Kirsten Margaret Iona, a particular name but of one universal family. There is a tune deep within the human soul that we are being invited to remember.

CHAPTER 3

The Rhythm of the Earth

Physicists now speak of being able to detect throughout the universe the sound that comes from the beginning of time. It vibrates through everything that has being. It is the sound of life's origin, even though in the ageless rocks of the sea or the countless fragments of meteorites that have fallen to earth over millennia, some of them even predating the birth of our solar system, the rhythm is so slow that we cannot audibly hear it.

I am sitting in the quiet of early morning in the high desert of New Mexico, having come for some days of writing, and I realize I cannot hear anything around me. The earth is in its winter stillness, the faint colors of dawn almost imperceptibly emerging in the east, the pregnant moon of last night having now dipped behind the great mesa to the west, and within the hour, the sun will be rising again in its glory. And I am reminded that at the end of this day, I will be able to see again a wonder that I witnessed this time last year, the sun's red globe hovering an inch above the western horizon at exactly the same time as the white moon in her fullness begins to climb in the east.

On my final day here last winter, I had hiked toward Chimney Rock, a sandstone column in the desert, separated now from the mesa that it was once part of, to gaze at the setting sun's glory. All my attention was on the burning glow in the west. But just behind me, I heard the swoosh-swoosh and call of a raven. And when I turned to look, I saw it: the moon in full splendor beginning its ascent. The bird had called my attention to what I was missing, a harmony of movement in the sky, a perfect rhythm between the brilliant sun setting and the enchanting moon rising. At that moment, I heard within me what the ancients call the "music of the spheres."

The Celts were familiar with this music. In the Hebrides of Scotland, it was common practice well into the nineteenth century for men to take off their caps to greet the morning sun and for women to bend their knee in reverence to the moon at night. These were the lights of God. They moved in an ancient harmony that spoke of the relationship of all things. And they witnessed also to the eternal rhythm between masculine energies and feminine energies that commingle deep in the body of the universe.

The Celts were familiar also with the practice of being guided by the creatures. The birds of the air, the fish of the sea, the animals of the earth had not lost their senses. They were viewed as still being alive to the deepest rhythms of creation and to the interrelationship between all things. And so whether on a physical journey into new territory or on a journey inward into a realm that felt strange and frightening, the help of the creatures was sought. Like the raven that called my attention to a harmony I had failed to notice, ancient Celts in their journeys of life watched for what the creatures remembered. And it was not always a gentle harmony that was being pointed to. Sometimes it is the wildness of God, the untamable energies of the divine within creation, that the creatures alert us to. And part of what we are taught is to approach the rhythms of the earth with awe.

A few years ago on Iona, I met a woman in her seventies who shared with me the story of her spiritual journey. She had grown up as a girl in the southern United States. It was their custom as a family to attend church every Sunday. One particular Sunday morning nearly sixty years ago, she was sitting in church when, halfway through the liturgy, a dog wandered into the sanctuary. It sauntered up the central aisle, sensing its way forward, until it got to the altar. There it stopped and began to sniff around. No, it did not do what you think I am going to say! It turned around and left. It did not like what it smelled. "That is when I left the church," the woman said to me. "It didn't smell right. It didn't smell natural."

It was a dog that guided this woman to see as a young adolescent that her religious environment did not smell right, that it had lost the connection between the natural and the holy, between spirit and matter, between God and creation. Her experience is eccentric in its details, but it is the story of countless numbers of women and men in the Western world today. They too have been born in the Christian household. They too no longer come to the family table. And it is because they too have not been truly nourished there in the past. Intuitively, they have known within themselves the goodness of the natural, the sacred origin of what is deepest in our nature and in all nature. Yet in so many cases, not only has that longing been neglected, but the religious fare they have been offered contradicts some of their deepest knowing and hunger for the goodness of creation.

The first teacher of historical significance in the Celtic Christian world, Irenaeus of Lyons in the second century, points to a profound integration between the sacred and the natural. Sometimes we think of Celtic territory being comprised only of Ireland, Scotland, Wales, Cornwall, and Brittany. But in the ancient world, the Celts spanned the whole of middle Europe, extending from Turkey in the east to the Atlantic coastline of Spain in the west. In 500 B.C., the vast tribal network of Celts included Galatia and Galicia and Gaul, all three of which simply mean "land of the Gaels." Only as the Roman Empire began to expand were the Celts pushed farther and farther west into what we now call the Celtic fringe of Britain and Ireland.

Irenaeus came originally from the Community of John in Asia Minor. He had been taught by Polycarp, the second-century bishop and martyr from ancient Smyrna (now modern Izmir in Turkey). Polycarp had in turn been the student of John the Beloved in Ephesus, the one who leaned against Jesus at the Last Supper and heard the Heartbeat of God. So Irenaeus and John are only one teacher apart. And we hear in Irenaeus in second-century Gaul some of John's favorite themes. "In the beginning was the Word," writes John in the prologue to his gospel (John 1:1). And all things have come into being through the Word. John is listening to the universe as an expression of God. It is spoken into being by the One from whom all things come. It comes directly from the heart of God's being. And in it we can hear the sound of the one Heartbeat.

So Irenaeus speaks of creation coming out of the very "substance" of God.[1] It is not as if the elements of the universe are fashioned out of a neutral substance. It is not as if creation is set in motion from afar. The matter of life comes forth directly from the womb of God's being. The glory of the sun rising in the east is the glory of God shining on us now and now and now. The whiteness of the moon, the wildness of the wind, the moisture of the fecund earth is the glow and wildness and moistness of God now. It is the very stuff of God's being of which we and creation are composed.

Irenaeus was writing in the face of two great falsenesses in his age. One was the falseness of the

Roman Empire, dominating the world with inhumanity, disregarding the sovereignty of nations, and inequitably ravishing the resources of the earth. The other was the rise of new spiritualities that looked above the matter of our being and beyond the body of creation for a *gnosis* or higher knowing that would save them from the rest of humanity and from the physicalness of their being. Both were viewed by Irenaeus as dangerous denials of the essential truth of the universe, that it is born of God's being and that it carries within itself the sounds of the sacred.

The two great falsenesses of Irenaeus' age are not significantly different from the falsenesses of our modern empires and religious devotions. Again the holders of military and economic might are betraying the sovereignty of nations and raping the earth, this time with even graver consequences. And again there are new expressions of spiritual belief that look away from creation for a truth that will separate believers from the mass of humanity and from the body of creation. Against these falsenesses Irenaeus teaches a gospel that leads us not into a separation from creation but into a harmony with the Heart of the universe.

Irenaeus uses a term that at first sight seems complicated. He speaks of Christ as "recapitulating" creation.[2] What do we do when we recapitulate something? We say it again. We repeat something that has already been said but in a way that brings into focus the essence of what was previously said but has been forgotten or obscured. Irenaeus teaches that Christ expresses the heart of the first work of God, namely, the work of creation, the deepest and most essential energy of the Creator. He is the recapitulation of the original utterance of God, not of something new or unrelated to the Word that calls all things into being.

Irenaeus then proceeds to use a term that is shockingly at odds with so much of what we have received in our Western Christian inheritance. He says that Christ recapitulates the "primal."[3] Christ reconnects us to the first and in that sense to the most truly primitive energies within the body of creation and the human form. How many of us have in fact been given the exact opposite impression, that Christ comes to lead us away from the primal, to overcome the elemental urges that course through our bodies and the body of the earth, that Christ comes to lead us into a transcending of the natural rather than reuniting us to the sacred root of the natural?

After Irenaeus, we find this same truth being pointed to in the words and art of the Celtic Christian world. The Celtic cross, which, as noted earlier, holds together its love of Christ and its love of creation by combining the images of the cross and the orb, invites us to see Christ and creation coming forth from the same point, both emerging from the Heart of God. Christ comes to reconnect us to that Heart, to the Unity from which all life comes. This is not to pretend that some of the deepest energies within the body of creation and the body of humanity have not become horribly confused and deeply distorted. It is, however, to celebrate that deeper than the confusions and distortions is the Sacred Core of Life, the Holy Source in which our harmony is again to be found. And it is to say that in the midst of our confusions and distortions of relationship, whether individually or collectively as an earth community, Christ comes not to lead us away from what is deepest in the body of reality and in the physicalness of our being but to root us again in the Holy Ground of All Being.

The great Celtic teachers repeatedly point to the fundamental truths of Genesis 1. It is used to remind us of our deepest identity, the image of God at the core of our being. It is also used to recall us to the essential nature of creation and of everything that has being. There is a phrase repeated after each day in the creation story. "And God saw that it was good. . . . And God saw that it was good. . . . And God saw all that had been made and beheld it was very good" (Genesis 1). Creation is viewed not simply as something that occurred at one point in the past. Creation is forever being born. It is forever coming out of the Womb of the Eternal, and God forever sees what is being born as sacred.

Not only is creation viewed as good, as coming out of the goodness of God, but it is viewed as well as theophany or a disclosing of the heart of God's being. Eriugena, the ninth-century Irish teacher, says that if goodness were extracted from the universe, all things would cease to exist. For goodness is not simply a feature of life; it is the very essence of life. Goodness gives rise to being just as evil leads to nonbeing or to a destruction and denial of life's sacredness. The extent to which we become evil or false is the extent to which we no longer truly exist. Eriugena and the Celtic teachers invite us to look to the deepest energies of our bodies and souls and to the deepest patterns and rhythms of the earth as theophanies of the goodness of God. And they invite us to see Christ as the One who speaks again this forgotten goodness, the Word that comes to us from the Beginning. He is the memory of the first and deepest sound within creation. It is an invitation to listen for the sacred not away from life but deep within all that has life.

Columbanus, the sixth-century Irish teacher, says that if we wish to know the Creator, we must come to know the creatures. He is teaching an attentiveness to the creatures as those who still remember the sacred rhythm of the earth. He is pointing also to a revering of the creaturely within us, of both our inner and outer senses, as rooted in the sacredness of being. We know that sometimes our outer senses fail us. We may think we are seeing something that in fact is not truly there, or our eyes may trick us into mistaking what we see for something else. We do not consequently stop using our senses. Rather we test them and use them discerningly and learn from one another how best to truly see. The same is true of our inner senses: like the woman who spoke to me on Iona, we need to pay attention to our deepest natural instincts if we are to recover the wholeness of life again.

During our years on Iona, we had a dog named Jo, which in Gaelic means "spark of life." And he was exactly that, a spark from the heart of life. Jo was a border collie, and he was true to his deepest instincts the whole of his life. He lived and breathed to round up, and if he was not allowed to round up sheep, he would try to round up children or tractors or even birds in the yard! His favorite day of the week on Iona was Wednesday, pilgrimage day, when sometimes with up to a hundred people we would walk the seven-mile route around the island reflecting on the journey of our lives and world together and praying for peace. Jo was excited from the beginning of the day. He knew it was Wednesday long before I took the shepherd's crook in hand to lead the walk. He was in an ecstasy of delight, rounding up pilgrims all day, at times looking almost berserk with joy as he circled endlessly in the heather.

But it was not frenetic running. His instinct was fine-tuned. It had a purpose, a goal that he was sensitive to. It was to hold us together. So as we approached in silence the hermit's cell at the heart of the island, now no more than a circular stone ruin from an ancient beehive hut used by Celtic monks for solitude, Jo quieted down, still attentive to anyone who might be straying or falling behind but intently quiet in his work. And when finally we all gathered in the circle of the hermit's cell for prayer, Jo would enter the cell, lie down at its center, and sleep. As someone who knows border collies said to me recently, "Of course he lay down. His work was finished. He had brought you together in a circle."

Jo's deepest instinct was to bring us into a unity. It is an instinct that has been bred particularly into border collies, but it is an instinct that comes from the Heart of Life, from the One from whom all things come. There is a longing within the whole of creation to form a circle again. It is a sacred longing. And I often think of Jo as a memory of that longing. The pain and betrayals of our lives may lead us to distrust or forget that holy instinct, but it is at the core of all that has being. And it is waiting to be reawakened in us, in the most intimate relationships of our lives and in the vast relationships of the earth's community.

Jo survived the transition from island life to city life when we left Iona, even though it led to some dangerous moments when Jo tried to round up city buses in Edinburgh! The instinct for unity is easier in some places than in others. And the challenge of spirituality is to keep alive the holy instincts that are awakened in us in sacred places like Iona and to be true to them in the busy and conflicted places of our lives and world. But the instinct is there, deep within.

There came a time, however, when Jo could no longer follow his instinct. He developed cancer. It was the year after our Brendan had become unwell. It was as if Jo had taken the pain of the family into himself. I remember the day on which he could no longer climb the stairs to our apartment in the city. I had to carry him, and as I lifted him, I began to weep. His eyes looked sad. How could this one who had lived to round us up leave us now when we were falling apart? By the time I reached the top of the stairs, I knew his time was near. I could not ask him to stay longer.

Shortly afterward, having arranged a time with the veterinary surgeon, I invited the family to come to the clinic for Jo's last moment. The only one who took up the invitation was our six-year-old, Cameron. The vet explained to us that she was going to give Jo an injection and that twenty seconds later he would take a deep breath, his last. We had already lifted Jo onto a table, and little Cameron's head was at exactly the same level. He leaned toward Jo to be as close as possible and to listen and watch intently for the last twenty seconds. Their faces were less than an inch apart. Cameron was fully present to Jo when he took his last breath.

The vet kindly offered to leave us in the room for a while. I suggested to Cameron that we say a prayer of thanks for Jo's spark of life and for his peaceful death. So we prayed and left in silence. As we began our walk home, Cameron said to me, "Daddy, I have a sore throat." So I said, "Why do you think you have a sore throat, Cameron?" And he replied, "I think it's because I'm wanting to cry." "I also have a sore throat, Cameron," I said. So we walked home together with our sore throats, and the family was waiting for us. And there we had a wake for Jo, with stories and tears and laughter.

What has happened to our instinct for unity? The creatures know the rhythm of the earth. They have not forgotten the oneness of which we are a part. So in the Celtic world, they are messengers of Christ, the One who comes to reconnect us to the Heart of Being. And they know when things do not smell right. They know when we have lost contact with the holy natural. The woman who shared her spiritual journey with me on Iona was not in the least apologetic for having followed the instincts of a dog sixty years earlier. She was, however, deeply sorry about having lived most of her life without spiritual community, without having others with whom to pray and sing, to share vision and tears, and to intimately work for the healing of our lives and world.

Part of what the creatures as messengers of Christ recall us to is that life is relational, that we will find well-being in and through one another as an earth community and not on our own, that we will find wholeness in the circle of unity and not in separation. This was part of the longing that I heard in the woman who spoke to me on Iona. She sensed that in the Celtic tradition, she would find an affirmation of her deepest instincts. She also sensed that she would find ways in which to begin to reclaim relationship in community. This beautifully natural but saddened woman is not alone. Her hunger is the hunger of men and women beyond number in our Western world. We are right to follow our sacred instincts for the natural. And we will be most deeply fed in our hunger when we find ways of doing this together. For it is together that we will most deeply hear the sacred rhythm. And it is when we are in a circle again that our work will be done.

CHAPTER 4

Empty Notes

We lived in southern England as a family in the late 1990s. The bishop of Portsmouth had asked me to bring the heart of Iona and its vision of linking spirituality and justice to one of the most densely populated cities in Britain. Portsmouth is a hard city. It carries painful scars from the past. Being a naval port, it has borne the brunt of military conflicts historically. It was burned to the ground by French and Spanish armadas. And during the Second World War, parts of it were bombed to smithereens by the German Luftwaffe. After the war, it was rebuilt in a hurry, apparently without use of the imagination, and ended up crowded and heavily paved.

We developed a great affection for the people of Portsmouth, but it was a difficult transition at first, especially for the older children, who had known years of running wild and free on one of the most beautiful Hebridean isles. Iona is an island that, as an Irish priest friend of mine once said, still has the freshness of the first day of creation. The grass is vibrant, the rocks glow, the beaches are pure, and the cattle are fat and sleek. Yes, it can be an island of wild wind and elemental storm, but in turbulence or stillness, Iona is a place where the sounds of the Beginning can immediately be heard. In Portsmouth, the cold concrete sounded empty.

The diocese provided us with an old vicarage in the city, and we called it Saint John's House. We wanted it to be a place of listening for the Heartbeat of Life. And we desperately needed to hear that beat ourselves in a strange city that felt forsaken. The vicarage had a yard. It had been neglected for years and was surrounded by barbed wire. But we sensed that this was where we were going to hear again the Garden of our Origins. We tore away the wire and began to hack at the briars and thorns that had taken over. Gradually we saw the traces of what once had been a beautiful garden. And I heard sounding repeatedly within me words from the book of Psalms: "God is in the midst of the city. It shall not be forsaken. . . . God is in the midst of the city. It shall not be forsaken" (Psalm 46:5).

There were many fine old trees in the yard. They formed something of a circle. I particularly loved the fig tree, massive with its many trunks and branches intertwined. I had cleared around the base of the tree, and its shade soon became a favorite place to sit with others and to teach. It was also the place where little Cameron took his midday nap. He was a babe in arms when we arrived in Portsmouth. Every day, we would place him in his baby carriage under the fig tree. It was close enough to the kitchen window to listen out.

One day, toward the end of Cameron's nap when I thought he would soon be waking, I went out to the yard. There he was, lying on his back in the carriage, fully awake but perfectly still. He was looking at the light dappling through the leaves of the fig tree. I paused to watch him. After a while, he lifted his arms toward the light in a type of response. I was witnessing a communion with the Glory that dapples through creation. And as I stood watching Cameron, I remembered, perhaps now the earliest memory of my life, doing exactly the same thing as an infant, lying under a tree watching light dapple.

The great Irish teacher John Scotus Eriugena taught that God speaks to us through two books. One is the little book, he says, the book of scripture, physically little. The other is the big book, the book of creation, vast as the universe.[1] Just as God speaks to us through the words of scripture, so God speaks to us through the elements of creation. The cosmos is like a living sacred text that we can learn to read and interpret. Just as we prayerfully ponder the words of the Bible in Christian practice, and as other traditions study their sacred texts, so we are invited to listen to the life of creation as an ongoing, living utterance of God.

The problem is that we hardly know the alphabet of that language. We have not been taught to read creation with the same devotion as we read scripture. But it is not because we have not been addressed. Some of our earliest memories of life are of being spoken to through creation. We remember as children lying on our backs in the grass gazing up into the infinity of the skies. We remember with open-eyed wonder watching light reflect off flowing water, whether in the purity of a country stream or in the gullies of a city street after rainfall. So it is not that we have not been addressed. And it is not that we are not being addressed now. It is that we have forgotten. And in many cases, it is because we have been educated out of listening to the sacred sounds of creation.

William Blake, the English poet, remembers as a boy seeing a tree filled with angels of light. He rushed home with excitement to share his vision with his father. And his father responded that if he ever told a lie like that again, he would get a good thrashing. There are ways of perceiving that have been beaten out of us. Our inner ears have been silenced, either because of modern materialisms that have stripped matter of its ancient music or because of religious dualisms that have separated the spiritual from the material. In both cases, the essential elements of the universe have become empty notes, devoid of sacred sound.

Eriugena invites us to listen to the two books in stereo, to listen to the strains of the human heart in scripture and to discern within them the sound of God and to listen to the murmurings and thunders of creation and to know within them the music of God's Being. To listen to the one without the other is to only half listen. To listen to scripture without creation is to lose the cosmic vastness of the song. To listen to creation without scripture is to lose the personal intimacy of the voice. And to listen to either is not to pretend that there are not difficulties in both. In the one text, we hear vengeance and hatred of the enemy that is as repulsive as the pain and apparently meaningless suffering that we read in the other. In the Celtic world, both texts are read in the company of Christ.

In the Celtic tradition, as noted, Christ is viewed as coming from the very heart of God and thus as disclosing to us what is at the heart of God's Being. Its high-standing crosses speak of the twin love of Christ and creation. They speak also of the devotion to the two texts, the big book and the little book. The artwork includes both scripture imagery and creation imagery. Sometimes, as is the case with the thousand-year-old high-standing cross of Saint Martin on Iona, the whole of the one side is devoted to scripture imagery and the whole of the other to creation imagery. Both belong to the cross design. Both are read in Christ. But in neither text do we passively receive whatever it says.

In both texts, we are listening for the Heartbeat that John heard in Jesus. In scripture, we are listening for the Heartbeat within the mixture of inspirations and confusions in the human soul. In creation, we are listening for God within the glory and birth pangs of the universe. We listen not away from the confusions and birth pangs but within them, as well as within the inspirations and glory. This is the place of Christ. And this is the place of the cross. What are the inspirations and confusions in our lives today? What are the glories and painful upheavals of our world and earth? We are being invited to listen within all of them for the Heartbeat from which our lives and the whole cosmos come.

It was after Christianity became the religion of the Roman Empire in the fourth century that the church began to teach its doctrine of creation *ex nihilo,* creation out of nothing. In response, Celtic teachers have said again and again over the centuries that creation does not come out of nothing. It comes out of God. The doctrine of creation *ex nihilo,* which has dominated so much of Western Christianity's approach to matter and to the earth, has given the impression that the essential elements of the universe were fashioned out of nothing by a distant Creator. It neutralized matter. It said that the physical universe, including our bodies, consists not of sacred substance but of empty substance. At best, matter existed to be the humble servant of spirit. At worst, it was the feared enemy of spirit.

Just as the doctrine of original sin was a convenient dogma for an empire set on dominating the world and dictating truth to the masses, so the doctrine of creation *ex nihilo* came into the service of a world power that was set on doing whatever it pleased to the earth. With impunity, it could ravish creation's resources for its own inequitable uses, and with the church's blessing, it could subordinate the energies within humanity closest to the earth, including the menstruating and birthing powers of the feminine. Just as the early Celtic teacher Pelagius was condemned for opposing the doctrine of original sin, so he was exiled for teaching that the gifts of nature are as holy as the gifts of grace and therefore to be justly distributed. So he was feared for teaching women to read and study scripture in the marketplaces of Rome, thus honoring the eternal feminine nature of wisdom and challenging the subordination of women that had already become the norm in the imperial church by the end of the fourth century.

And what have the empires of the world been allowed to do since then? And what are they being allowed to do at this point in time? If there is to be a new birthing of Christ for today that serves the growing awareness of the one-ness and sacredness of the earth, and if there is to be a new birthing within the Christian household of a wisdom that will fully serve the recovery of the divine feminine as well as the divine masculine within us and among us in our lives and world, then we must learn to hear the Heartbeat within the matter and deepest energies of the earth. Then we must say unequivocally that the notes of the universe are not empty. They are filled with God.

This will radically change the way we touch matter, the matter of human bodies, the matter of the earth, the matter of the body politic and how we relate as sovereign nations. And it will set us free to move in relationship, rather than in fear, with the deepest energies that pulse within us, within our bodies, and within the earth. The disastrous consequences of the doctrine of creation *ex nihilo* are many, in terms of what we have done and are doing to the creatures and the resources of the earth, but among the most painful implications are how we have approached the deep physical and sexual energies of our being.

Again it is in the fourth century, during Christianity's transition to being the religion of the empire, that we find a marked fear dominating the approach to sexuality. Instead of our natural sexual attractions and longings for physical union being regarded as among the deepest and holiest expressions of the dance of the universe, increasingly they were treated as opposed to the rhythm of God's Being. Instead of God being viewed as the Unity from which all life comes, and therefore as engendering in us holy desire for union in soul and in body, a tragic separation was introduced between the spiritual and the physical. And the church began to articulate a belief in the perpetual virginity of Mary, even though the early

New Testament manuscripts make it perfectly clear Jesus had brothers and sisters. Similarly, the church began to teach that chastity was a higher spiritual path than marital union.

It is interesting to note that in John's gospel, particularly cherished in the Celtic world, Mary is never referred to as a virgin. She is a mother. And in no other gospel tradition is she more honored, but it is because she is a mother, the conceiver and bearer of sacred life, not because she is a virgin. And the first family reference to Jesus in John's gospel is "son of Joseph of Nazareth" (John 1:45). There is no need to contravene the elemental rhythms and patterns of procreation in the natural world to say that the Holy has been conceived among us. At the birth of every child, the Holy is born. In the conception of every creature, the Sacred One is at work. The gospel of Christ reveals not a foreign truth, that God is born on earth only through a denial of the natural or via supranatural action. The gospel of Christ reveals the dearest and most hidden of truths, that we are what Christ is, born of God, and that at the heart of every human being and every creature is the Light that was in the beginning and through whom all things have come into being.

To see Christ as revealing the deepest truth of our being, rather than embodying a truth that is essentially foreign to us, is not to belittle the work or the person of Christ. It is not to reduce his uniqueness and mystery to our preconceived notions of what it is to be human. It is rather to recover and lift up our vision of what is at the heart of the human soul and the body of creation. It is to remember that we and all things are born of the eternal womb of God. We honor Christ not because he embodies an exclusive truth, a truth that pertains only to him. We bow to Christ because he reveals the most inclusive of truths, the truth we have forgotten or lost sight of within us and between us as an earth community, that the very elements of our being and the whole universe come forth directly from God's Being.

By the fifth century, the church had moved to such extreme lengths in distancing the natural from the holy that there are absurd descriptions of the conception of the Christ child in Mary's ear rather than directly into her womb. Contact lower than the neck presumably would not have been worthy of the Holy Spirit! If such descriptions were not so lamentable, they could simply be left behind as laughable. If they had not done so much damage, we could just describe them as deluded. But they represent the tragic severing of the spiritual from the physical and of the holy from the sexual that has worked untold havoc in the hearts and lives of countless men and women through the centuries and continues to do so today. Of course, our sexual energies are infected with selfish desire and have been linked to some of the most horrific acts of domination and abuse in the history of humanity, but it is precisely because we have forgotten the holy root of sexuality that we continue to forget how it is to be truly expressed.

The doctrine of the virgin birth is a corollary of the doctrine of creation *ex nihilo*. And it could be seen also as a corollary of the doctrine of original sin. It assumes that we are essentially opposed to God instead of being essentially of God. And it assumes that the deepest notes of our bodies are bereft of sacred sound rather than quivering with divine tones that long to be part of birthing the Holy. If we are to serve the growing creation consciousness of today that knows the sacredness of matter, then as a Christian household we must find ways creatively to name the falseness of many of the doctrines we have received. If by *virgin* we mean "perpetually chaste" rather than simply "young woman," as in the Isaiah prophecy (Isaiah 7:14), perhaps we should no longer use the word. If, on the other hand, we look to Mary as conceiver and birther, as pure expression of the eternal feminine energy within us opening receptively to the holy seeds of new beginning, we will have found a way of loving Mary again and offering her as a great treasure to the world for today.

In John's gospel, there is another Mary, Mary Magdalene, who is equally cherished. Part of what we are hearing today in the rediscovery of ancient manuscripts that open up lost perspectives of Jesus is an excitement about the possibility that Mary Magdalene was Jesus' partner in life. All we can say at this point in time, of course, is that she might have been. But the excitement is rooted in the desire to find ways of radically affirming again the essential goodness of sexual union and the sacredness of the deepest patterns of nature. We do not in fact have to look beyond the bounds of our New Testament canon to see signs of the cherished relationship between Jesus and Mary Magdalene. In John's gospel, she is the first to whom the risen Christ appears.

It is in a garden that Christ comes to the one who is longing for his presence. At first, Mary Magdalene thinks he is the gardener, which in a sense he is. He comes from the Garden of our Origins. He comes to nurture what is deepest in us, our genesis in God. But it is only when he calls her by name that she recognizes him. There is no such thing as a general sighting of Christ. He appears in the intimacy of relationship. He comes from deep in the Garden of our Being, where each one of us is called by name. He comes to reconnect us to the Sacred Root of our bodies and souls and to the Holy Ground of all that has being.

Eriugena, in commenting on the story of the first garden, the Garden from which all life comes, reflects on the biblical passage in which God is described as walking in the garden at the time of the evening breeze.

Adam and Eve have become false to themselves and to the One who is at the heart of the garden. They are hiding and have covered the nakedness of their being. In the Genesis account, God says to them, "Where are you?" (Genesis 3:9). Eriugena adds that God is forever walking in the garden of our beings, asking why we are hiding, why we are covering our nature, why we are living at a distance from our truest origin. From the genesis of our soul, he says, God is asking, "Where are you?"[2]

Where are we? Where are we as individuals today? Where are we in the most important relationships of our lives? Where are we as religious traditions and nations? Where are we as an earth community? Are we in hiding from our true nature and from the deepest notes of life's Garden? Are we cutting ourselves off from the Voice that still sounds from Eden, inviting us to respond to our name, our deepest identity, Adam "of the ground," Eve "womb of life"?

When I stood in the yard in Portsmouth looking at Cameron under the fig tree, I received a memory from the earliest days of my life. It was calling me back to a way of seeing that I had become distant from, of gazing at the Light that is dappling through all things now. Not surprisingly, the memory came to me through a child. Cameron had not forgotten. He was still naturally alive to the Music of the Garden. And he saw its notes dancing through the leaves.

CHAPTER 5

The Sound
of Love

L ast year, during a visit to New Mexico, I had a conversation with a Pueblo leader. We stood gazing out over the high desert at sunset. The western sky was on fire, and the desert floor and distant mesas were glowing ocher and red. We watched creation's lifeblood pulse through the land and sky around us. After a while, I spoke, at some length, about the Celtic practice of listening for the beat of God within all things. When I finished, he smiled and said, "Yes, we too know the Heartbeat." Then on a drum that rested against his body, he began to beat the ancient rhythm of the earth that his ancestors have known forever, di-dum, di-dum, di-dum, di-dum.

I felt embarrassed at having held forth about something he knew so deeply. But even more than embarrassment was my sense of the humility of the man in whose presence I stood. He would not have claimed to be my teacher, but through a simple drumbeat, he not only shared his people's ancient belief but also led me into an experience of listening that I will never forget. I was no longer simply thinking about the beat or talking about it. I was knowing it in my being, hearing its vibrations within me, feeling it in my body and in the body of the earth. And I realized that the humility of this man was grounded in what we were hearing. It was pure gift, vast and powerful as well as intimate and tender.

Apart from being a slow learner, I do not know why the connection between drumbeat and Heartbeat had not been more obvious to me. Perhaps it was a deeper, more physical way of knowing than what my Western Christian tradition has shaped in me. But maybe, more painfully, it was the blindness to native wisdom that has been such a marked feature of my cultural inheritance. I grew up as a boy in Canada, a native land, with a deep love of its lakes and rhythm of seasons and skies but with no real knowledge of its first people. In my case, the inherited prejudice was largely unspoken and unconscious, but it was pervasive. There had been no expectation fostered in me to look to the First Nations people for wisdom. In fact, quite the contrary: I had been trained to see little beyond the wreckage of their culture.

Only somewhat recently in my life has this way of seeing been radically challenged. Early in 2002, I was giving a series of talks in Prince Albert, Saskatchewan. My host sensed that there was common ground between Celtic spirituality and the ancient insights of the Cree Nation. So he spoke to the native leaders at the Silver Lake Reservation, and they invited me to participate in their sweat lodge. I realized that it was a great honor to be invited, so I approached the time with some trepidation. And had I not been quite so ignorant of what a sweat lodge is, I would have approached it also with some terror!

Twelve of us, including nine native elders, gathered in the early morning by the lodge. At its highest point, this rounded structure, framed with curved branches and covered with blankets and hide, stands about five feet tall and ten feet in diameter. A flap was opened on the side, and we bent low to enter. At its center was a pit into which hot rocks from an overnight fire were placed. We sat in a circle, stripped, one bare shoulder pressed against another in the round. When the flap closed, we were in total darkness.

For my sake, some words of welcome were spoken in English by the oldest elder. He then moved into Cree, sprinkling onto the rocks pieces of sage that sparked alight and scented the lodge. Then the chanting, rattling, and drumbeat began. In no time, the space heated up, and I felt our bodies bowing together toward the earth to seek its coolness. With a sprig of spruce dipped in water, the leader began to splash the burning rocks. With each splash, steam gushed up from the pit. Again and again he splashed. And now we were no longer simply bowing toward the earth; we were hugging it, desperately embracing the cool ground because our bodies were on fire with heat. Cries, unintelligible to me, were coming from the others in the circle, and I felt I could not endure it physically any longer. After a final shout, the flap came up. It was the end of the first of four sessions, one for each of the earth's directions.

We had begun with the west, the setting of the sun and the season of autumn, earth's time of dying. We moved next to the north, to winter and the season of barrenness. After each session, which lasted about twenty minutes, I was invited to step outside for a breath of fresh air, although most of the elders remained seated inside. At the end of the second session, standing next to the flap in the freezing cold of winter, I thought I was going to faint. And it occurred to me that I did not know where to place my body. Should I fall into the snow, I thought, which was about minus 40 degrees Fahrenheit, or back into the lodge, with its 150-plus temperatures? So I said to the youngest elder, about my age, standing beside me, "I think I'm going to be sick. I'm going to black out." It was at this point that the young elder, who had previously been hesitant to speak about the ritual, chose to offer some wisdom. The more I came to know him, the more I realized that it was not that he did not want to share with me. It was that he did not want to place himself above me as my teacher. But now I needed help, so he spoke.

"Your body is trying to tell you that it's in control," he said. "It doesn't like what is happening, so it's trying to bale out. But we don't believe the body is the center of our being. And when you go back into the sweat lodge, perhaps your mind will tell you that it is in control and will produce a convincing reason for you to leave. But we don't believe that the mind is the center of our being either. Here we are seeking to be renewed in the ground that is deeper than our bodies and minds, the One Ground of Life from which we and all things come." He then offered me a cup of ice-cold water. And the words and the water mingled in me to give me strength. The sessions that followed were hotter still, with fresh burning rocks added from the fire, but the young elder had opened in me the way to continue and to be blessed.

At the end of the fourth round, the south, summer, the season of green and new life, we lay, still stripped, on the naked floor of an unheated cabin nearby allowing coolness to reenter our bodies. We lay in stillness as a bowl of stewed berries and honey was passed from one person to the next in a circle of communion. Never has my body supped such sweetness from the earth! After a while, I broke the silence with a question: "What was the phrase you were repeating as you chanted at the beginning of each round?" There was no reply for at least a minute. And long after I had given up hope of being answered, the oldest elder responded. "We were praying for you," he said, "and for your people." My people, the people who had so wronged his people. My people, the people who could not hear the sound of love and wisdom in his people.

For many months after this experience, I could not speak about it without either weeping or being close to tears. I still do not understand why entirely, but I do know that I was in touch in a new way with the pain of a terrible brokenness that we have inflicted on an ancient people of wisdom. And I know also that in the prayers of that sweat lodge, and in the heart of that elder, I heard the sound of love in a way that further awakened my desire to change and be part of the healing of the earth. Within that love, I heard a great strength of soul. Julian of Norwich says, "The soul is highest, noblest, worthiest when it is lowest, humblest, and gentlest."[1] In my native brothers, I experienced the strength of humility, of being close to the ground or the "humus" of our being. And I saw in a new way what Julian means when she says that Christ is the one who connects us to the "great root" of our being.[2]

Dame Julian, the fourteenth-century English mystic, came originally from the ancient Celtic territory north of Norwich, closer to Whitby, where centuries earlier, the Celtic mission had been displaced by the powerful imperial mission of Rome. We know little about her life and the influences that played on her spirituality, but it is clear from her writings that the Celtic resonances are strong. "God is our mother as truly as God is our father," she says.[3] We come from the Womb of the Eternal. We are not simply made by God; we are made "of God."[4] So we encounter the energy of God in our true depths. And we will know the One from whom we have come only to the extent that we know ourselves. God is the "ground" of life.[5] So it is to the very essence of our being that we look for God. It is to the Humus of Life that we turn to find our deepest identity.

God "is in everything," writes Julian.[6] God is "nature's substance," the very essence of life.[7] So she speaks of "smelling" God, of "swallowing" God in the waters and juices of the earth, of "feeling" God in the human body and the body of creation.[8] And she insists, as the Celtic tradition has done since its inception, that nature and grace are one. They move in harmony. "Grace is God as Nature is God," she says. "Neither of them works without the other."[9] Grace is given to save our nature, not to save us from our nature. It is given to free us from the unnaturalness of what we have become and done to one another and to the earth. Grace is given, she says, "to bring nature back to that blessed point from which it came, namely God."[10] It is given that we may hear again the deepest sounds within us.

What Julian hears is that "we are all one."[11] We have come from God as one, and to God we shall return as one. And any true well-being in our lives will be found not in isolation but in relation. She uses the image of the knot, so loved by Celtic artists over the centuries, to portray the strands of time and eternity intertwined, of the human and the creaturely inseparably interrelated, of the one and the many forever married. Christ's soul and our soul are like an everlasting knot. The deeper we move in our own being, the closer we come to Christ. And the closer we come to Christ's soul, the nearer we move to the heart of one another. In Christ, we hear not foreign sounds but the deepest intimations of the human and the divine intertwined.

And for Julian, the key to hearing what is at the heart of the human soul is to listen to our deepest longings, for "the desire of the soul," she says, "is the desire of God."[12] Of course, many of our desires have become infected or overlaid by confusions and distortions, but at the root of our being is the sacred longing for union. It is to this deepest root that Christ leads us. Our soul is made "of God," as Julian says, so it is grounded in the desires of God. And at the heart of these holy desires is what Julian calls "love-longing."[13] It is the most sacred and the most natural of yearnings. The deeper we move within the human soul, the closer we come to this divine yearning. And the nearer we come to our true self, "the greater our longing will be."[14] It is, Julian says, a "wound" of longing.[15] For if it is not healed or nourished, it becomes irritated and inflamed. If our longings for love in life, whether individual or collective, whether physical or spiritual, are not reciprocated, we experience torment within ourselves, just as we know agony in love at times in the most mutually self-giving relationships of our lives.

It is this that Julian sees something of in her series of dreamlike visions or revelations of Christ when she was a young woman in 1373. She calls them "showings." And as the word suggests, they are about the bleeding and pain and discharges of longing and love and new births in life. At one point, as she lies desperately ill, she sees so much blood in her vision of Christ that she says if it had been real blood, her bed would have been soaked to overflowing. But the blood of Christ that she sees is not about payment to God for sin. It is about the very nature of love. It is a revelation or a showing of what it means to long for love and to live for love. If we wish to avoid suffering in our lives, we should shut down to the deep love-longings of our soul. For it is because we love that we are in grief when our loved ones die. It is because we love our children that we are in pain when we see them suffer. It is because we love our nations that we are in agony when we see them being false to themselves. And it is because we love the earth that we weep at its body being violated. Julian hears Christ thirsting on the cross. She sees him bleeding from his open side. These are for her "showings" or "revelations of divine love." They lead her to hear the deepest sounds of the soul, our thirst for love, our longing for union.

There is a connection between desire and conception, just as there is a connection between conception and birth pangs. To be in touch with the deepest desires of the soul and the love-longings that stir within us will lead to new conception in our lives and relationships. These will in turn lead us into both the joy and the pain of new birthings. In one of her visions, Julian sees that Christ's countenance is a combination of pain and sorrow on the one hand and joy and bliss on the other. What births happen without pain? And what are the new births of delight waiting to happen in our lives and world that also will be costly? We are invited to be in touch with our deepest desires and to know in their unfoldings the pangs of new beginnings.

I shall always remember the primal scream of my wife, Ali, at the birth of Rowan, our first child. It was a sound I had never heard before, but it was deeply familiar because it was coming from a place close to the heart of life. It came forth not just from Ali's physical and spiritual depths. It came from the beginning of time. It was deep and prolonged like the history of the universe. In it, I was hearing the birth of every creature and the great ruptures of earth's labor. It is a scream that also echoes within us when we contemplate what we must pass through as individuals and nations if we are really to experience new beginnings in the most broken places of our lives and world today.

In the book of Revelation, John, in one of his dreamlike visions, sees a woman clothed with the sun, with the moon at her feet and crowned with stars. She is crying out in the pangs of birth. It is a powerful image of the eternal feminine, of the conceiving and birthing energies deep in the body of the universe and deep in the human soul. But there is another image in John's dream as well. It is the portent of a great red dragon, multiheaded and horned. It waits in front of the woman to devour her child as soon as it is born. It is the shadow, the capacity for false and destructive energy within us and between us that obstructs new birthings and chooses death and destruction over life. There is a third image, however. It is Michael, the mighty archangel of God, leading an angelic host of light in a cosmic battle against the dragon. Michael, whose name means "one who resembles God," is a messenger of heaven's presence. He embodies the grace that has the power to save the deepest birthing energies of our nature.

In Julian's "showings" she receives the promise that "all shall be well and all shall be well and all manner of things shall be well."[16] This is not a naive optimism in Julian. Her visions are full of blood and suffering. She knows the destructive energies of dragon forces within us.

And she sees the agonies of new birth. The promise is not that she and those whom she loves will avoid pain. The promise is that all shall be well. And the promise is based not on a downplaying of the destructive powers that move within us and within the universe but on her vision that the love-longings of God will never cease and that they will never be erased from the human soul.

Jesus says, "When a woman is in labor, she has pain because her hour has come" (John 16:21). What are the longings within us today, in our lives individually and collectively? What are the yearnings that are stirring in our souls and families and in the most important relationships of our nations and earth community? And what is the labor, especially the birth pangs of labor, that will be part of any new birthing of wholeness in our lives, of healing among us as religious traditions, of unity between us as nations, of recovered harmony within us as a single body of creation?

Julian sees in one of her visions that "there is a deed which the Holy Trinity will do on the last day" that will make all things well.[17] It may be that literally she imagined a last day for the universe, perhaps the Day of Judgment, of setting all things right. But her words point also to something ultimate or absolutely critical at the heart of life that holds within it the power to heal and transform. She does not see what the deed is, but given what she says about the soul being greatest when it is humblest, it is a deed or posture of such staggering humility that it has the power to shake the foundations of the universe back into wholeness. "Without humility," Julian says, "we cannot be saved."[18] What are the acts of humility, of being reconnected to the Ground of Life's Oneness again, that will heal us and our world?

A few years ago, my research into John, who in his dream saw the woman clothed with the sun in the agony of giving birth, led me on a type of pilgrimage into John territory and especially to John's tomb in Selçuk, Turkey, close to ancient Ephesus. My wife and I, not for the first time in our lives, managed to get lost and wandered by mistake into the garden courtyard of a mosque in Selçuk. The imam welcomed us and asked about our visit to Turkey. And when he learned that I was a minister, he bowed to me. "You are a minister of Christ," he said. He then invited us into the mosque, where we exchanged blessings. It was the imam who then showed us where the burial place of John was, just up the hill from the mosque.

As I climbed toward the tomb, I could not stop thinking about the humility of this teacher who had bowed to me. It was the same posture of soul that I had encountered years earlier in the old Cree elder from Saskatchewan. And I realized that their humility of spirit was in no sense a betrayal of their religious convictions. Quite the opposite. It was the truest mark of their spirituality. And they were inviting me to be true to the heart of my tradition, true to the Humble One. They were inviting me to hear in Christ's humility the strong sound of love, the sound that has the power to change us. "Without humility," says Julian, "we cannot be saved." Without humility, we will not find together the Holy Ground from which we come. Without humility, we will not hear again the deepest stirrings in the soil of our soul, the sound of love.

CHAPTER 6

Paying the Piper

Not long ago, I met a woman who had inherited some jewelry from her mother. Among the pieces was a cross, and she did not know what to do with it. The teachings she had received about the cross of Christ either bewildered her or did not relate to her deepest experiences of life and relationship. But at the same time, she did not want to throw it away or lose it. In fact, a part of her saw it as so precious that she ended up placing it under the floor boards of her house for safe-keeping.

This woman is not alone in her confusion of relationship with the cross. Countless numbers of men and women in the Western world have found the church's traditional teaching about the cross either perplexing or offensive, especially the suggestion that Christ's death is a type of payment for sin. Who exactly is requiring payment? Is there some cosmic legal system at work, more complicated even than our earthly judicatures, that somehow needs to be satisfied?

It does not take long to get turned around in this maze of legal-theological argument. The result is that many within the Christian household have simply chosen to place the cross under the floor boards of their religious consciousness. They neither talk about the cross nor employ it personally as a significant symbol in their lives. And then there are the many, both within and on the edge of the Christian household, who continue to do things like give and receive crosses as gifts, even wearing them close to their hearts. But often this represents not an acceptance of religious orthodoxy but an intuition that the cross somehow relates to love. In both cases, there is a type of awareness that the cross is a precious part of our inheritance. But what exactly are we to do with it? And what exactly does it mean?

A number of years ago, I delivered a series of talks in Santa Fe on Celtic Christianity. Among my listeners was an elderly woman, highly educated and theologically aware. At the end of the series, she said to me in all seriousness, "Philip, the Celtic tradition is very interesting, but it isn't Christian, is it?" When I drew breath, enough to try to respond generously, I found myself wondering, How could she possibly say this? One has only to look at the ancient art forms of Celtic spirituality to detect a deep devotion to Christ and to the cross. Similarly, one has only to read, even cursorily, the prayers and poems of this tradition to note that Christ and the cross are inextricably present. So what did she mean?

The longer I listened, the more I realized that what she was saying was, "This doesn't sound familiar." And she is right. This does not sound familiar. And one of the things we do not hear in Celtic spirituality is the doctrine of substitutionary atonement, a dogma that has dominated the landscape of Western Christian thought and practice. Like so much else in our imperial Christian inheritance, it is linked with the doctrine of original sin. There are two assumptions behind this thinking. First, God requires payment, like a piper that can be paid to change his tune, from judgment to forgiveness. And second, we are so sinful that we cannot make a worthy payment. So a substitute is made, which God himself provides: Christ, the perfect sacrifice.

It is easy to ridicule the logic of a doctrinal system in which God offers God payment. Much more important is to try to name what the preciousness of the cross is for those of us who have intuited that it is dear to our inheritance but have ended up hiding it under the floor boards. Part of a new birthing of Christ for today is to ask what obstacles block the birth canal and to remove them. And if we are discovering, as I believe we are, that there is much in the doctrine of substitutionary atonement that is opposed to our deepest experiences of forgiveness—namely, that forgiveness by its very nature is absolutely free—then we need to find new language to speak about the way in which Christ leads us into the experience of forgiveness at the heart of life and into the practice of forgiveness in our lives and relationships, both as individuals and as nations. And part of what we are invited to do in dialogue within the Christian household on this matter is to look for the positive roots of belief even amid the gnarled and distorted branches of old imperial doctrine.

I once led a retreat for chaplains of the British Armed Forces in Germany returning from service in Iraq. The venue was a former Hitler Youth camp, which made for a complicated spiritual atmosphere in a fine old building on the edge of the ancient forest of Luneburg. The retreat was silent with the exception of three meditative talks each day. I waited until my final talk on the last day to introduce questions about the doctrine of substitutionary atonement. A few hours later, when we had come out of silence and were gathered at the bar for a drink, one of the chaplains stormed up to me and said, "When you criticized the doctrine of substitutionary atonement that way, I nearly got up and punched you in the face." What followed could not be described as an edifying conversation.

I had difficulty sleeping that night. I did not feel right about the way I had responded. And I found myself wondering, What is it about a theory that makes one brother want to punch another brother in the face? So I made a point of looking for him at breakfast the next morning. And I made sure I did not call his belief in substitutionary atonement a theory. Otherwise, he might well have punched me in the face. Instead I suggested that everything we say about Christ and the cross is at the end of the day only an attempt to say what cannot be put into words. And I asked if our real common ground was not in fact that we had both experienced forgiveness in relation to Christ.

He too had had a sleepless night. And the conversation that followed was very different from the previous evening. We were now listening to one another. And one of the things I heard from him was that he had had a profound spiritual experience of forgiveness and that he had experienced the forgiveness of God as pure gift. What the language of substitutionary atonement said to him, however, was that although forgiveness is free, it is not cheap. I agree. Forgiveness is the most costly of gifts because it involves the sacrifice of the heart. When we forgive another, we offer our heart to the person. So it can cost us everything. It was this that my chaplain brother saw in the cross of Christ, the heart of God.

Who are we prepared to give our hearts to? Who are the individuals who have wronged us or the nations or communities that are at war with us? It is to these that Christ calls us to open our heart. This is the way of making peace: "peace through the blood of the cross," Saint Paul calls it (Colossians 1:20). We make peace by offering our hearts. Forgiveness is free. We can offer it and receive it only as pure gift. Yet forgiveness is costly, for we can participate in it only to the extent that we open ourselves. But forgiveness is not about payment.

Never. It is about a free and costly opening of ourselves to one another in ways that have the power to heal and transform us.

As much as I am able to see some light and warmth hidden in a doctrine that otherwise seems opaque and inhumanly cold, what I see much more clearly is the damage that has been done in the lives and relationships of countless individuals and the punitive norms that have been established in "Christian" nations whereby, when wrong is done, someone has to pay. The doctrine of substitutionary atonement is not only opposed to our deepest experiences of forgiveness in life; it perpetuates the notion that what is at the heart of God, and therefore what is at the heart of the human mystery, is judgment, not love. And judgment must be satisfied, paid for, before love can be offered. The piper needs to be paid to change his tune, even though he provides the fee himself. But his default mode is judgment.

The elderly woman in Santa Fe had concluded that Celtic spirituality was not Christian because it did not include the doctrine of substitutionary atonement. This was another version of the chaplain wanting to punch me in the face. I was throwing the baby out with the bath water. What is it, then, that the Celtic tradition is pointing to in its love of Christ and its devotion to the cross? Why is there so much cross imagery in its art and prayers? What accounts for the great high-standing crosses that are rooted deep in the landscape of the ancient Celtic world?

Celtic spirituality is more poetic than doctrinal. Belief is pointed to rather than defined. And the ancient Celtic mission did not have a theological headquarters, like the Vatican in the imperial mission, to impose orthodoxy from the center. So there is no neat doctrinal phrase in the Celtic world to contrast with substitutionary atonement. But if one phrase had to be chosen to point to the difference, it would be the title of Dame Julian's series of dreamlike visions of Christ, "The Revelation of Love." Her visions are filled with harrowing depictions of the blood and suffering of Christ on the cross. But they are never about payment. They are always about revelation or "showings," as she calls them. They are a disclosure of God. "Whoever sees me sees the One who sent me" (John 12:45), Saint John describes Jesus as saying. And in the Celtic tradition, the cross is the greatest showing of God.

It discloses the first and deepest impulse of God, self-giving. It reveals that everything God does is a pouring out of love, a sharing of lifeblood. And so the whole of creation is an ongoing offering of self, a showing of the Eternal Heart that is pulsing with love in the life of all things. Not only does the cross disclose love, but it also discloses the cost of love. To offer the heart is to offer the self. And so the cross, in addition to being a revelation of the nature of God, is a revelation of our true nature, made in the image of God. It reveals that we come closest to our true self when we pour ourselves out in love for one another, when we give our heart and thus the whole of our being.

One of the greatest teachers in the Celtic world was Aelred of Rievaulx, who was born in northern England in the twelfth century and became the foster son of David I, king of Scotland. He taught that God is not our Judge but our Lover. Judgment, in and by itself, has no power to profoundly change us. It can frighten or inhibit us, but it cannot transform us. Only love transforms us, for only love has the power to change our hearts. Any transforming experience of judgment in our souls, therefore, in which we come to see and desire what is right (*jus*, the Latin root of *judge* and *judgment*) is based on an awareness that we have been untrue to the Beloved. And what this awareness awakens in us is a longing to change, whether in our relationship to the Lover in creation or in our relationship to the Lover within ourselves and within one another.

And just as God is Lover, longing for union, rather than Judge, demanding union, so, for Aelred, Christ is companion of our soul rather than ransom for our soul. Aelred takes as his ideal of relationship the love between Jesus and John. He describes them as looking to each other's heart—John listening for the Heartbeat of

God in Jesus and Jesus showing the secrets of his heart to John. We find in John's gospel the theme of mutual indwelling: "Abide in me as I abide in you," says Jesus (John 15:4). Being present to the heart of the other, looking with love to the essence of the other—this is what releases the truest depths in one another.

Jesus says that from our heart will flow "rivers of living water" (John 7:38). Who are the people who release the deepest currents of our being, the people who look to the heart of who we are and set free our richest inner streams? Aelred teaches that it is through one another that Christ kisses us into wholeness. There is the physical or "corporeal kiss," he says, "the meeting of lips," the moist intimacy of giving and receiving in love. And there is the "spiritual kiss," he says, the "mingling of spirits," the merging of hearts in which we find that we are one.[1]

I have been blessed with companions of my soul, people who have kissed me into greater wholeness in my life. Companions of the soul may be sought intentionally in our lives with structured times and disciplines of looking to one another's heart to release depths that hitherto we have not known. But a companion of the soul may also be pure gift, someone who has been given to us through the most natural of life's relationships: friend, brother, sister, lover, father, mother, son, daughter.

One of the most important companions of my soul is my eleven-year-old son Cameron. I realize that he may soon feel the need to partly withdraw his heart from me as he moves through adolescence into a more defined sense of self. I hope that he will not have to withdraw himself too much, but I will wait for him as my father waited for me to open my heart again. Cameron blesses me with companionship at a deep level in my life because again and again I find him looking to my heart.

Last spring, he accompanied me to the premiere celebration of an Earth Mass for Peace that I've written in collaboration with a Vermont composer friend, Sam Guarnaccia. On the way home in the car, Cameron said to me in all innocence, "Daddy, have you ever won the Nobel Peace Prize?" What a beautiful thing to ask, even though he knows full well that if there were a family prize for peace, I would take sixth place, and there are only six of us in the family. But he looks to my heart, and in so doing, he further releases in me streams of yearning for life and creativity and peace. How can we do this for one another? How can we look into one another's hearts in ways that will open up the hidden wellsprings of life and new beginnings?

Another companion of my soul, at the other end of the age spectrum, is my father. He has always been a strong presence in my life. He was a firm disciplinarian for us as children growing up, providing well-defined boundaries for the family, which was probably a very good thing, although it rarely seemed so at the time. But this is not why he is companion of my soul. His greatest strength in our relationship has been his willingness to weep with me at the most critical moments of my life. He has the gift of tears. At every major point of struggle or joy in my journey, including times of pain and delight in my own fathering, he has looked to my heart. And his tears have opened streams of new life in me.

I had an epiphany moment in my early adolescence. It came through someone else who looked to my heart, my mother's mother. She lived with us when I was a boy. Granny Ferguson, from Banffshire in Scotland, was a presence of unconditional love in my life. I could do no wrong in her eyes, even though she knew full well I was a mischievous "scallywag," as she called me. But she looked to my heart. I knew that to her I was precious and would always be precious. I have since come to realize the same thing about my mother, but I was an adolescent at the time, so the realization came through my granny. I knew, beyond a shadow of doubt, that there was nothing I could do that would make my granny not love me. And so my epiphany moment came when I realized that Granny was more loving than the God of my religious tradition.

I had been given the impression that God somehow required payment to forgive, whereas I knew that my granny would never need to be paid to forgive me. The doctrine of substitutionary atonement, and the general religious atmosphere that surrounds that dogma, struck me as a violation of everything I most deeply knew about love, that it is entirely free. Who are the people who have truly loved us in our lives? Could we imagine them ever needing to be paid to forgive? In my mind, it was like the prostitution of God, payment for love. I did not have theological tools at that time to unpack the implications of this realization, but I knew deep within myself that there was something wrong with my religious inheritance.

A number of years ago, I flew into the Asheville airport on my way to the Montreat Conference Center in the mountains of North Carolina. I had been instructed to take a cab that was going to be shared with a couple who would be dropped off en route. In the car, we got talking about one another's journeys and the various things we were about to do in North Carolina. One subject led to another until eventually we began to speak about substitutionary atonement, as one does in taxicabs! The woman in particular sensed that I was saying something very different, a bit like the older woman in Santa Fe. The conversation became awkward in the close confines of the cab. And part of me wished I was walking to Montreat! Then she shouted, "But what about the blood?" What about the blood? To speak about the cross as revelation of love rather than payment for sin is not to suggest that this is merely a show. This is real blood. This is real self-giving. Jesus knew full well the cost of loving his nation and his religious tradition the way he did, enough to weep over the falseness of the city he loved and to cleanse the injustices of the temple at its core. This is real suffering at the hands of a corrupt religious leadership and an inhumane empire that would not tolerate the challenging implications of the law of love. But it is not a payment to God; it is a disclosure of God. It is not a purchasing of love; it is the manifestation of love.

One of the most ancient symbols of Christ in the Celtic world is the salmon. We find it in the earliest strands of Celtic Christian art and poetry. Even in the pre-Christian Celtic world, it is a favorite image, associated especially with true knowledge and wisdom. Of course, the fish had been a symbol of Christ in the earliest centuries of the church, but in the Celtic world, it specifically became a salmon. So the ancient symbolism for wisdom merges with the Christian symbolism for love, and love and its longings are viewed as the deepest expression of wisdom. The salmon, strong and glistening with vitality, swims hundreds of miles in the open sea and climbs thousands of feet in the torrents of mighty rivers to give birth to new life. And in spawning new life, it dies. Christ, the Salmon of Wisdom, the One who gives himself for the birthing of new life.

In the weeks leading up to the writing of this chapter, my father-in-law died after a long struggle with dementia. It has been a tear-washed time in which we have been able to remember the diamond essence of this one whom we have loved. One of our most cherished memories of him is standing waist-deep in the northern rivers of Scotland fishing, waiting for the salmon to leap. He once caught a fifteen-pound salmon the same week his ten-pound grandson was born. So by the time word reached home, he had become the grandfather of a fifteen-pound baby!

We have been able to remember his passion for the river of life and his belief that its deepest current is love. Normally a restless man, he would wait patiently for hours in the river for the salmon to leap, waiting also, I believe, to reconnect with the deepest vitality within himself. When the great fish came, it came freely in unbounded desire to spawn new life. There was no other reason for it to swim against the tide. There was no other reason for it to give all its glistening strength to the journey. It came unbidden, with unbounded longing. In the Celtic world, Christ is this bright, blessed, beautiful Salmon. Love comes freely from the heart of life, with costly longing.

CHAPTER 7

The Hymn of
the Universe

As many people as there are in the world, so are there ways of experiencing the Presence, for we and all things carry the Presence within us. Often we use the word God as if we know exactly what we are talking about. It is as if God, which really is a metaphor, becomes the proper name for the Unknown, and in using it, we think we have named that which is beyond names. Always what cannot be said is greater than what can be said. And the same is true for each of us and for all things. What cannot be uttered about another is always greater than what can be uttered. The tendency to name and define the Ineffable has given rise to the tendency also to standardize our experience of the Presence. This not only limits what we have to say, but it also narrows our expectations of where and when and how we will encounter the sacred. And for vast numbers of people, including many of my friends and family, it silences even the thought of being personally addressed at the core of our being by the Unknown.

In my early teens, during that period in adolescence when a torrent of confusing energies begins to whirl within us, I had an experience that I did not share for over thirty-five years. I woke up in the middle of the night and was aware of the presence of Christ. He did not say anything to me verbally, but his posture spoke powerfully and reassuringly. It was a dark room, so I was able to see only the outline of his form. He was seated on a chair immediately next to my bed. His body was inclined toward me. His head was tilted. He leaned forward with total attention. My experience was that Christ was looking to the heart of my being, with love.

The next day, when I went to school, my best friend looked at me and said, "Philip, what has happened to you?" I am ashamed to say that I did not tell him. And I did not tell anyone for decades. Only very recently in my life have I chosen to share this experience. I think I understand why. I am not a mystic. I was not given to mystical experiences as a boy, nor have I been since. And I was not a particularly devout teenager. The experience did not come as a result of devotion. It was pure gift. And I see it now as a glimpse into the Personal Presence at the heart of life. But I had been given the impression that it was only certain people who had such experiences, and they were "insiders" with Jesus. And then there was the rest of humanity.

I did not have tools to make sense of this middle-of-the-night experience, and it seemed too intimate to speak about. But I certainly did not feel I was part of an exclusive company. So the only religious language available to me felt inadequate. Instinctively, I knew I was not separate from the rest of humanity. But I did not know how to speak about the experience. So I silenced it and hid it away in secret for most of my life. I have since come to realize that a great many people experience the presence of Christ, both within and outside the Christian household, and that countless others experience the Unknown without name or by other names, and that the experience is one of Love. It is vitally important that we hear from one another so that our fragments of vision, which in isolation can seem strange, together might become a fuller picture of the deeply personal nature of the universe.

In the Celtic world early in the twentieth century, a new vision of Christ appeared simultaneously in the lives of two great Christian teachers. One was George Macleod, founder of the modern-day Iona Community in Scotland. The other was Pierre Teilhard de Chardin, the French mystic, scientist, and priest. At the core of their vision was an experience of Christ's presence. But for both of them, this was not a presence that was separate from humanity or that separated them from humanity. Rather it was a presence of Love at the heart of creation that led them into a deeper union with the human soul and into a sharper sense of earth's oneness. As Macleod later said, "Christ is vibrant in the material world, not just in the spiritual world."[1] Or as Teilhard put it, "At the heart of matter is the heart of God."[2] The deeper we move in the body of creation and in the inner landscape of the human soul, the closer we come to the Presence. Christ carries a tune that is at the heart of matter. It is not a tune that separates us from the rest of the world. Rather it leads us into the deepest sounds of the hymn of the universe.

This new vision of Christ emerged not in the beauty of a Scottish Hebridean island or in the grandeur of the Loire Valley in France but on the front lines of the First World War in Europe. Sometimes the caricature of Celtic Christianity is of a Wordsworthian romanticism that idyllizes the countryside from the comfortable safety of the city. Macleod, as a British soldier, and Teilhard, as a stretcher-bearer in the French army, experienced the Presence in the midst of the horror of what humanity is capable of doing to itself. Human bodies were being blown to bits, and the French countryside was being ripped apart by explosive violence. It was here that Macleod and Teilhard experienced Christ as the suffering presence of Love.

What are the brokennesses in our world today? What are the battlefields among the nations and the gaping wounds of creation's body? What are the discords in our communities and the struggles in the most important relationships of our lives? It is here that we are invited to look for the Presence, as well as in the infinite beauty and wildness of creation and the limitless imagination and longings of the human spirit. Sometimes it is especially when the minds and bodies of those we most love and the soul and fabric of the nations and lands we most cherish, are torn apart that we remember the unspeakable beauty at the heart of life. As Teilhard wrote after the harrowing Battle of Ypres in 1915, "More than ever I believe that life is beautiful."[3]

It was during a leave of absence, as Macleod traveled home from the front, that he became aware of the presence of Christ. It was not a foreign presence. It emerged immediately from the suffering and struggle of nations that Macleod was part of. The train was crowded, packed with soldiers, some of whom, like him, had been decorated for acts of bravery and others of whom were wounded. So overwhelmed was he by a sense of the Presence that he knelt down in the moving railway carriage and gave himself to Christ. Always a man of action, he could not wait until the end of the journey. He knew what he had to do, so he made his commitment there and then. And it changed the course of his life. Instead of being a soldier for his nation, he was to become, as he later called it, a *miles Christi*, a soldier for Christ, committed to nonviolence.

I came to know George Macleod in his later years. I realize now that part of his greatness was that he did not mind repeating himself. And he lived until he was ninety-six, so he had plenty of opportunity to repeat himself. One of the things he loved to say was "Matter matters, because at the heart of the material is the spiritual."

What we do to matter, therefore, is at the heart of our spirituality, whether that be the matter of our bodies and how we touch one another in relationship individually and collectively, whether that be the matter of the earth's energies and how we handle and share its goodness, or whether that be the matter of the body politic and how we approach one another's sovereignty as nations. These are holy matters. And it was because Macleod believed that the Presence is deep within matter and that creation is the Body of God that he committed himself and inspired others to what he called "nonviolence of heart and action." Tirelessly, he preached peace. In fact, he was one of the most aggressive pacifists that the modern world has known!

My last conversation with George Macleod, if *conversation* is the right word to describe a telephone exchange in which I think all I said was "Hello," was shortly before he died in 1991. I had been asked to write a column for the *Guardian*, a national newspaper in Britain. The occasion was August 6, both the Feast of the Transfiguration and Hiroshima Day. Macleod had always been passionate about Christ as Light of the world, not just spiritual light but physical light. He refused to separate the unseen from the seen or to divorce spirit from matter. So the article I wrote was pure Macleod. I spoke of light as transfiguringly sacred but pointed also to the way in which the sacred can be twisted into destructive energy, as we did in dropping the atomic bomb on the citizens of Hiroshima in 1945.

Macleod read my article in Edinburgh that day. And at the age of ninety-six, being less clear than he formerly was, he thought the article was his, which in a sense it was, although I happened to have written it. But thinking it was his writing, he instructed his personal assistant to run off three hundred copies so that he could send them out to his friends. Just before he sent them out, however, his daughter, Mary, came in and said, "This isn't your article, father. This is Philip's." So immediately he picked up the phone to call me on Iona. And this literally was the content of our conversation after I answered: "Newell, Macleod here. Such a good article, thought it was my own." Click.

It does not seem that Macleod ever met Teilhard de Chardin. But they were brothers of the same vision. And their journeys were remarkably similar. Teilhard was born in 1881, of ancient Gallic ancestry in France, and was educated in Lyons. In his autobiography, he remembers as a boy being "drawn to Matter," or more specifically, "to something which shone at the heart of Matter."[4] But having been reared in the traditional piety of a Roman Catholic family, he lacked tools for integrating his experience of matter with his religious inheritance. In fact, he had been given the impression that matter was "no more than the humble servant of spirit, if not, indeed, its enemy."[5] Consequently, religious devotion meant little to him at this stage, and as a young man, Teilhard entered what he describes as his pantheistic years. Everything in the universe seemed equally sacred to him, but there was no sense yet of a Presence at the heart of matter.

This awareness came suddenly for him in the midst of the collective turmoil of soul that was engulfing Europe in 1914. As he agonized over what was happening between the nations and personally despaired about the direction of the world, he heard himself being addressed by Christ, "*Ego sum, noli timere* (It is I, be not afraid)."[6] He experienced these words (from Saint Matthew's gospel) as coming not from afar or from above the anguished journey of the nations. He heard them within himself, as coming from the heart of matter and from the deepest place in the human soul. And these words set him free for the rest of his life to delve deeply into matter, whether that was the dark matter of the earth and its hidden secrets or the mysterious matter of the human soul and its eternal stirrings. And in both he looked for the Presence. "It is I, be not afraid."

In an essay titled "Cosmic Life," Teilhard later wrote, "There is a communion with God, and a communion with earth, and a communion with God through earth."[7] His religious tradition had taught him that there is a "communion with God." His natural instincts had taught him that there is a "communion with earth." But his experience of Christ taught him that there is a "communion with God through earth." It was to this communion that he devoted the remainder of his life. In his paleontological work as a scientist, he would dig into the earth. In his theological work as a priest, he would search the depths of the human soul. And in both, he was seeking communion with God.

It was in the brokenness of Europe and the bloody trenches of the front lines that Teilhard woke up to communion with God through earth. During Easter week 1916 at the Battle of Dunkirk, he wrote, "The more I devote myself in some way to the interests of the earth . . . the more I belong to God."[8] It was as he cared for the wounded, it was as he felt the shock of the earth around him, bombs blasting craters out of trampled vineyards, that he came to see most clearly the sacredness of creation's body. He saw that what we do to one another as nations and what we do to the earth as a human race is what we do to the Presence of Love. And with almost unbelievable tenderness, he addresses Christ and creation in one breath: "I love you, Lord Jesus," he prays at Dunkirk. "You are as gentle as the human heart, as fiery as the forces of nature, as intimate as life itself. . . . I love you as a world, as this world which has captivated my heart."[9]

What do we do when our heart is captured by love? And what do we do when the children we love, when the friends who always have been there for us, when the nation that is our homeland, when the parents who have birthed us—what do we do when they suffer? We know our oneness with them. And we long for their well-being as if it were our own. Teilhard's love of Christ and love of creation, which he holds inseparably together, led him to know his union with Christ and creation. Christ for him was the "Soul shining forth" through the universe.[10] He comes to see that his true center will be found not within the limited confines of his own individuality but at the heart of life. It is there that he will find his truest identity, in the Heart from which all hearts come. And it is there that he will find his well-being, in relationship with all things, not in separation.

Teilhard coined the concept of *excentration* as his way of saying that we find our true selves outside of ourselves or that we find our true center in the heart of one another and at the heart of all life.[11] Yes, we also find the Presence deep within ourselves, but the experience is of encountering the Presence that is the Heart of all life. The deeper we move within our souls, the closer we come to the soul of one another. And the closer we move to the heart of all life, the nearer we come to the heart of our own being. Teilhard recognizes this as a costly path, for it is to let go of the notion that we can find well-being in isolation, whether as nations or religious communities, whether as individuals or species. And so the cross of

Christ becomes for Teilhard our "true image."[12] It is in no sense an expiation or payment to God. It is a revelation of the Presence at the heart of the universe. It reveals the greatest truth, that we will keep our heart only by giving our heart away, that we will find ourselves only by losing ourselves in love, that we will gain salvation only by spreading our arms wide for one another and for the earth, and that we will be saved together, not in separation.

The Presence that I was aware of in the middle of the night as an adolescent was a self-giving presence, the figure of Christ inclined toward me in love with total attention. Julian of Norwich says in relation to her series of dreamlike encounters with Christ that they are not hers. They are ours, she says, for "we are all one."[13] They belong to the human soul. If I had known that, I would have had the language to speak about my experience. If I had known that, I would have found ways of sharing it as a blessing for us all instead of hiding it away as a private experience. But I did not know it.

Instead, what set me free to speak about my experience of Christ was an awareness that came to me one night last year in New Mexico. I was having a writing week in the high desert. The earth was in its winter nakedness. The trees surrounding the portal of my little dwelling were still stripped bare. And as I sat out under the open skies, and the stars in their brilliance seemed closer to me than I had ever experienced them, I was aware that the poplars with their willowy branches were inclining toward the portal. Then everything I could see in the darkness of that night and in the infinite stretches of space above me, the shimmering planets and glistening galaxies—they were all inclining with Presence. And I knew it was for us all, and I was set free to speak.

An experience of Presence. A hymn that fills the whole universe. A melody that continues whether we are listening or not. A song that is heard especially amid tears and confusion and brokenness. Sitting up in bed in the middle of the night as a young adolescent. Sitting on a portal under the open skies of New Mexico nearly forty years later. In addition to the pain that I carry in my own psyche and family and nation, I was especially aware that night of the body of pain that is held in the people and landscape of the high desert of New Mexico. One wave after another of incoming people doing violence to the other. European nations ravaging the resources and ancient cultures of native tribes. And within forty miles of where I sat, the Los Alamos National Laboratory, where the bombs that killed hundreds of thousands of Japanese were designed and tested. And where bombs that could destroy the family of the earth continue to be produced today.

It was in the midst of earth's pain that Macleod and Teilhard listened. They heard the hymn that is as ancient as the universe and as new as today's fresh birthings of love. It is the hymn that reminds us of the harmony at the heart of creation, the hymn of cosmic sounds and intimate whisperings. It is the hymn in which one theme is heard in an unending infinity of voices. It is the song of Presence. *Ego sum noli timere.* It is the hymn of Self-giving Love that sets us free to be part of the healing of the universe.

CHAPTER 8

Broken Cadences

There is a little sanctuary in Chimayo, New Mexico, dedicated to healing. Generations of women and men have traveled to this shrine, often in pilgrimage mode, seeking miraculous cures for themselves and their loved ones. It has a type of beauty to it, with its *retablo* style of art, its colorfully dressed statues of Jesus and Mary, and its ocher-shaded sand reputed to have healing properties. But the last time I entered it, I realized I was standing in a religious nursery, with its brightly colored childlike art, its liturgical range of pretty dresses for Jesus and Mary, and its ecclesiastical sandbox of holy dirt.

I do not mean to suggest that there is not a place for nurseries in life. It did feel safe and sheltered. It had a type of innocence and even playfulness about it. The problem relates much more to whether or not our Western Christian traditions generally have graduated from the nursery. The atmosphere of "father knows best" still prevails, even though for many people that has been expanded to include women ministers. The effect is pretty much the same, however. Responsibility for handling and interpreting the mysteries is left to the "safety" of those in charge. And the impression that the sanctuary's dirt is more holy than all other dirt is perpetuated in various ways, even though that usually takes the form of the bread and wine of the sacrament or the letters and words of scripture, being considered more holy than the rest of matter.

But the most dangerous aspect of the nursery paradigm is the notion that healing and salvation can be received in isolation from one another as individuals and communities and nations. Given what we now know about the oneness of the body of reality, what does it mean to seek healing and salvation? How can I claim to be whole as a father if my son is suffering? How can we claim to be well as a people if other nations are in pain? How can we be healthy as a human race if the body of the earth is infected? To offer the hope of salvation to the people of our religious traditions and imply, implicitly or explicitly, that this might not include the rest of humanity and the rest of the earth contradicts everything we now know about the interrelatedness of life and well-being.

When Julian of Norwich receives her inner assurance that "all shall be well, and all shall be well, and all manner of things shall be well,"[1] part of what she is hearing is that she will not be well and that each one of us will not be truly well, including our families and nations and entire species, until all things are well. There are certain brokennesses in our lives and relationships and world that will not be healed until we are all healed. We are so deeply part of one another, and of all things, that it is meaningless to speak about wholeness in separation.

Wholeness comes in relationship, not in fragmentation. Until we move together again in harmony with the hymn of the universe, our songs of salvation will sound like broken cadences torn from the whole.

In the ancient Celtic mission, from the fourth to seventh centuries, the pattern for worship was to gather around high-standing crosses in the context of earth, sea, and sky. The emphasis was that creation itself was the Sanctuary of God. And it included all things. Not until the imperial mission triumphed in Britain at the Synod of Whitby in 664, and in the centuries following, do we begin to find the mighty four-walled stone religious structures that we now so strongly identify with Christian worship.

On Iona, I was grateful that we had both. We had the ancient high-standing cross of Saint Martin to remind us of the unbounded place of the sacred. And we had the thirteenth-century Benedictine Abbey in which to seek shelter and community together. But we need to find ways of being reminded that our religious sanctuaries are at best side chapels onto the great cathedral of creation. Otherwise the impression is given, as historically it has been again and again, that God is somehow more present within the four walls than in every other place and that the time for meeting within the four walls of our religious sanctuaries is somehow more sacred than all other moments and that the people who gather within the four walls are somehow more holy than all other people. Tragically, the impression has been created that we seek well-being and salvation by separating ourselves from creation and from the rest of the world rather than by more deeply integrating ourselves.

By the end of the First World War, Teilhard de Chardin had taken his final vows for the Jesuit priesthood and was back in Paris working on a doctorate in geology. Having experienced the presence of Christ on the front lines, in both the glory and pain of creation and the human journey, Teilhard found the hard boundary lines of religious orthodoxy limiting and claustrophobic. He expressed his frustration to a friend: "I believe that the Church is still a child," he said. "Christ, by whom she lives, is immeasurably greater than she imagines."[2]

Not surprisingly, such sentiments did not endear Teilhard to his ecclesiastical superiors. They felt threatened by a prophetic vision that anticipated the earth consciousness of today. As early as the 1920s, Teilhard was saying in Paris what someone like Dietrich Bonhoeffer later asserted in Nazi Germany in the 1940s when he spoke of a Christianity come of age, a Christianity that needs to graduate from the nursery of a religiosity that tries to shelter from the complexity of the world's struggles and the mighty birth pangs of the earth and the human soul, a Christianity that looks, as George Macleod used to say, "not for soul salvation but for whole salvation," that seeks our well-being in relation to the well-being of the entire earth community rather than in isolation from it, a Christianity that can be part of leading the new consciousness of earth's oneness instead of being irrelevant to it or opposed to it.

Teilhard also wrote to a friend in the 1920s of the need to free "our religion from everything about it that is specifically Mediterranean."[3] And the doctrine that he saw as a fundamental obstacle to the emerging consciousness of earth's oneness was the "Mediterranean" or "imperial" doctrine of original sin. It opposed the deepest energies of the human soul to God, including the deepest energies of creation. Instead of being taught to find our wholeness together in the shared Ground of all being, we were being taught to look away from the earth and our common inheritance to a salvation that would separate us from the rest of the world. Teilhard was summoned to his religious superiors in Lyons in 1924 to account for his teachings. "They want me to promise in writing," he said, "that I will never say or write anything against the traditional position of the Church on original sin."[4]

The upshot was that the church in its wisdom sent him to China, to get him out of the way. But little did they know what the East would do to Teilhard. Officially, he was sent as a paleontologist and was part of one of the most exciting scientific expeditions of his time, the discovery of Sinanthropus, or "Peking Man," which dated human origins to as early as 500,000 years ago. But he was exposed in a new way also to the mysticism of the East. It opened him further to a sense of the oneness of life. It provided him with ways of seeing that underlined the unity rather than the separateness of things. "Without mysticism," he later wrote, "there can be no successful religion."[5] The mystical path he saw as opening our inner eye to the Oneness of which we are a part. It reminds us that our healing will come in relationship, not in isolation. Teilhard began to speak of "the confluence of East and West."[6] He envisaged a marriage between the insights of the Western world, with its cherished ideals of individuality and distinctness, and the deep sensibilities of the East, with its intuitions of mystery and union.

But always for Teilhard true union sets us free to be radically ourselves. True union differentiates. We know this in the most important relationships of our lives. It is those with whom we are most intimately united in mind or body or soul who have the greatest power to release our uniqueness. And so for Teilhard, a marriage between East and West represented a commingling that would further free us. It was not a conformity to one another that would bind us into a limited uniformity of belief and practice. In the deepest of meetings in our lives, whether as individuals or cultures, whether as nations or wisdom traditions, we are being invited to discover through one another what on our own we have not been able to know.

For Teilhard in China, this was happening at a personal as well as philosophical level. In the wisdom of the East, he was becoming aware of the eternal attraction of feminine and masculine energies within the body of the universe. "Everything in the universe is made by union," he wrote, "by the coming together of elements that seek out one another."[7] And so he begins to speak of the "fragrance" of the feminine deep within the matter of the earth and the human soul.[8] It is that part of us, and of all things, that stirs a passion for union. It is that part of us that longs to move in relationship and to find new beginnings by coming closer to the core of one another.

In the midst of these unfolding awarenesses, Teilhard entered a life-changing relationship with Lucile Swan, an American sculptor from Iowa, who also was living and working in Beijing. For ten years, they met together almost daily, to converse and share deeply. But it was not an uncomplicated relationship, if there is such a thing! Teilhard realized that through Lucile, he came closer to the heart of his own soul. There were riches in his depths that he discovered only through her and through their shared love.

But Lucile wanted the relationship to be complete, including the sexual. She wanted them to give themselves entirely to each another. As she later wrote, "Please don't think I meant just sex, although that is very strong. It would make a bond between us that would add a strength that I believe nothing else can give. However, that is only a part. I want to be with you when you are well and when you are ill. Go see beautiful things with you and walk through the country. In other words, I want to stand beside you always, to laugh and play and pray with you. Don't you realize what a big part of life that is, and how that is what is right and normal and God-given?"[9] Teilhard, however, had already committed himself to another path. But it was not because he believed the celibate path was higher than sexual union. Celibacy was the distinct way in which he was giving himself to the world he loved. He might also have given himself to the life of the world through Lucile. But he had to make a choice. So the gift of love that they had received was also a gift wrapped in pain.

To move toward the heart of another, whether that be a man or a woman, whether that be another nation or a different religious tradition, is often to enter the anguished territory of making decisions that would not have to be made if we had remained distant and separate. Whenever we follow the longing for union that stirs deep in the human soul, we begin a new journey to know exactly what form that longing should take. We experience this again and again in our lives when we open to the "fragrance" within another or within another's culture and religious inheritance. To say that the desire for union is sacred is not to say that it is simple. And to say that Christ shows us the way of union is not to say that it comes without cost.

In Beijing in the 1930s, Teilhard expresses his belief that what the incarnation reveals to us is that we "can be saved only by becoming one with the universe."[10] Christ shows us the way of becoming one with matter, one with humanity, one with creation. He shows us the way of union rather than separation. But what exactly does it mean for us today to follow Christ into oneness with the earth and with humanity? What does it mean to commit ourselves to being one with our neighbor or with those who suffer or with the life of other nations or with the wisdom of other religions?

In 2006, as the Community of Casa del Sol was being born in the high desert of New Mexico, I met Rabbi Nahum from Santa Fe. We were in conversation for only a few minutes before realizing we were brothers. We recognized each other's soul. And I began to tell him about another rabbi I had known from Jerusalem, who had visited us on Iona years ago, taught us Torah, and shared communion with us. During our conversation, I noticed that Nahum's eyes were, like mine, moist with emotion, for we knew that we too wanted to find ways of being fed together as brothers. The next day, Nahum called to say he wanted to teach with me at Casa del Sol.

Our mornings that summer were spent in the courtyard of Casa del Sol, where sixteen of us explored what it means to love Christ and to follow him into a deeper union with the human soul and with the body of the earth. Then in the early evenings, we would sit under the cottonwood trees with Nahum as he asked questions of the Hebrew scriptures for the world today. And we found that the searchings of the morning were being met in the teachings of the evening and that the questions of the evening were throwing light on the studies of the morning. As Rabbi Nahum later said, "When Philip teaches, it goes in Christian and comes out Jewish." I agree, but in reverse. Nahum's teachings were feeding my love of Christ. It is in relationship that we find our wholeness, not in separation. For we are one.

Toward the end of our first week together, I asked Nahum if he would preach at the communion service on Sunday. And I gave him a good gospel text. Amusingly, at the beginning of his sermon, he explained that Christians have been wanting Jews to come to church for centuries. The difference here, he said, was that he had been invited to come to church to be Jewish. After he preached, communion was celebrated, and Nahum participated fully. We shared together the bread and wine of the earth, not the church. We ate and drank to nourish the human soul, not the separateness of our religious identities. As we shared communion, I was not simply weeping; I was sobbing. The centuries of division and brokenness that I carry within myself were being washed away. It was as if my heart was being shaken to its foundations, where we are one. And there we were being fed.

Teilhard returned to Paris at the end of the Second World War. In the East, he had become more deeply convinced that our salvation is to be found together, not in separated strands. We must "let the very heart of the earth . . . beat within us," he said.[11] It is one rhythm that sounds at the core of our being. And it is in relationship with one another and with all things that we will most clearly hear the sacred beat of the Presence. Yet back in Europe, Teilhard found that his religious tradition was still pursuing a path that set out to liberate the "saved" from the rest of humanity and that promised a salvation that would somehow transcend the earth. Christ was being presented, at the end of the day, as a deserter of creation and a forsaker of the human journey. He had come to strike up a tune at odds with the universe rather than recovering the hymn at its very core.

It was particularly the religious leadership of his church that Teilhard criticized. Even in China, he had been saying that we must "save Christ from the hands of the clerics so that the world may be saved."[12] Teilhard prophetically saw that humanity was at a "change of age."[13] He announced a uniting vision of reality that helped prepare the way for greater unity among nations and dialogue between religious traditions. He foresaw a change of age that has grown today into a consciousness of earth's oneness that is unparalleled in the history of humanity, despite the painful and destructive reactions to that vision that continue to threaten the very future of our planet. It was Teilhard's awareness of an emerging change that led him to long for what he called a new birthing within the Christian household. "After what will soon be 2000 years," he said, "Christ must be born again."[14]

Again, however, his ecclesiastical superiors felt threatened by his vision. They did not want him teaching in Europe. So for a second time, they sent him into exile, this time to the United States. But his longing for a new birthing of Christ did not wane. As he wrote to the general of his Jesuit order at this time, "Never has Christ seemed to me more real, more personal or more immense."[15] It is this threefold vision of Christ—real, personal, and immense—that is not only typical of the Celtic tradition's devotion to Christ and to creation but also announces the shape of a rebirthing of Christianity for today.

There is a longing in the human soul for what is real, for what connects with the new vision of reality that recognizes that all things are interconnected. There is a longing in the human heart for what is personal, for what addresses the most intimate core of our being in its eternal yearnings for love and union. There is a longing in the human spirit for what is immense, for what expands our vision further into the unboundedness of the universe. As Teilhard said, when we hear the Heartbeat of God, whether in our own soul or in the heart of another, whether in the body of creation or in the vast expanses of the cosmos, we experience ourselves being called "by name."[16] Our place of deepest and most personal identity is addressed. The voice is intimate and immense. It is both personal and vast.

Love of Christ and love of creation—these, said Teilhard, are the "twin poles" of the spirituality of the future.[17] Believing in Christ and believing in the earth—these are the axes of faith that will lead us again to the very heart of the universe. They are spirit and matter conjoined. They are passion and fecundity interwoven. They are personal presence and infinite expanse at the same time. And if we allow ourselves to be called by name by the Presence at the heart of "every blessed thing,"[18] as George Macleod referred to the matter of the universe, we will be changed. And we will discover again that together we belong to the one ancient Harmony. "It is this I now see with a vision that will never leave me," wrote Teilhard, "that the World is desperately in need of at this very moment, if it is not to collapse."[19]

Teilhard died on Easter 1955 at the Jesuit house in New York. He died alone and relatively unknown. There were ten people at his funeral, and only one person accompanied his body for burial. Yet fifty years later, the memory of this prophet was celebrated at the United Nations in the company of thousands. He lived and named the longings of the human heart that are stirring within us now. Devotion to Christ and devotion to the Earth were one in his vision, in ways that anticipated a new birthing of spirituality for today. On his desk in New York was found a prayer, titled "My Litany," that he had written and was clearly using on a regular basis. Its final words read, "Heart of Jesus, Heart of Creation, unite me to yourself."[20] Many of us have known a love of Christ and a love of the unfolding earth in our lives. Most of us have not known how to hold the two together.

At the *sanctuario* in New Mexico, I experienced discomfort at a religiosity that sought healing in isolation from the rest of humanity and in opposition to nature. I realize now that the discomfort was not primarily about that little place of pilgrimage with its colorful expressions of heartfelt piety and personal sacrifice. My discomfort was much more about the Christian household at large and whether or not we are going to find ways of integrating devotion to Christ with devotion to the earth, whether or not we are going to find ways of seeking wholeness as a single body of creation and as one human soul rather than as separate strands.

Perhaps the most hopeful note about that little sanctuary in Chimayo is its most famed feature, its holy dirt. If we can find ways of holding together again our love of Christ with our love of the earth's dirt, not just religious dirt or Christian dirt but all dirt, including the most basic elements of the universe, we will find ourselves part of a new birthing. Then we will find ourselves hearing again the deepest harmonies of the universe within us and within all things. Heart of Jesus, Heart of Creation, unite us to yourself.

Postlude

I am writing the final words of this book on the Isle of Iona, where for me it all began. Iona over the centuries has been a place of new beginnings. It was here in the sixth century that Saint Columba began his mission to Scotland. Having sailed from Ireland in penitent exile from his native land because of a battle he had incited, Columba experienced on this little island a grace of new birth that was to become also a birthing of Christianity for the whole nation. And since then, countless pilgrims have come, also carrying within them the failures and hopes of their lives and nations, seeking here new beginnings for themselves and peace for the world.

It was on Iona in the late 1980s that I became deeply aware of the lost treasure of Celtic Christianity. In the ancient prayers of the Hebrides, especially in the collection known as the *Carmina Gadelica* ("Songs of the Gaels"), I found prayers that had been chanted for centuries at the rising of the sun and the setting of the sun, invocations for blessing at the birth of a child or the death of a loved one, rhythms of praise for the tides and the turning of seasons, and songs of thanks for planting and harvesting earth's fruits. These were different from the prayers I had grown up with in my Western Christian inheritance. The context was creation rather than church. Love of Christ and love of the earth were woven inseparably together. And I saw in them hidden gems for the journey of the human soul today.

Here on Iona I find myself wanting more often to pray in the ruins of the nunnery than in the rebuilt abbey church. And I am not alone in this desire. Although all of the attention historically has been focused on the reconstructed thirteenth-century Benedictine Abbey, a place of masculine spirituality, rather than on the ruins of the neglected Augustinian Nunnery of the same period, a place of feminine spirituality, we are in the midst of a shift. When I first arrived on Iona in the late 1980s, the nunnery was not even included in the weekly pilgrimage around the island. Now it is not only a prominent stopping place on the Iona pilgrimage route but also a place where countless individuals pray in solitude and where groups of pilgrims can be found offering impromptu rituals and songs for the healing of the earth. What does this say? What is it about the nunnery that is speaking into the heart of the human journey now?

The nunnery sits open to creation. Whether in sun or in storm, whether in the open skies of a clear morning or the infinite stretches of space at night, in the nunnery one is aware of the elements, of birdsong, of ivy-leafed toadflax growing amid the red granite stones of the ruined structure, of unbridled wind. It is this that so many of us are looking for in our spiritual journey today, a connection between spirit and matter, the ancient bond between the wild and the sacred, an openness in relationship between prayer and the cosmos.

But the nunnery is not simply creation. It is not like praying in an open field of heather or on a rocky mountaintop. The nunnery has been a place of relationship, of intentional community, and devotion to Christ and the cross. It has been a place where people have scrubbed potatoes together, shed tears at the news of births and deaths, and sung communal songs of the soul to the One who is beyond names but who is known as Love. It is this that many of us are seeking in the spiritual journey of humanity today, a vision of relationship, a sense of community at joyful and pain-filled transition points in life, and through it all a conscious yearning for the Living Presence.

But the nunnery is also a ruin. It is a place that reflects the brokenness of our lives and our world, as well as the failure of our religious institutions. It is a place that states clearly that we have not got it right and that we do not yet know exactly what shape the emerging spirituality of today will take. It is also a place that resounds with the neglect of the feminine that has so crippled our Western cultures and spirituality. It is this that many of us are longing for in the spiritual journey of the world today, a recognition that our imperial religious inheritance is collapsing and that we desperately need to reintegrate the mystical, intuitive, and earth-related fragrances of the feminine if we are to be alive to the deepest yearnings of the human soul.

George Macleod, the founder of the modern-day Iona Community, is more associated with the rebuilt abbey than with the ruined nunnery. But he would not have claimed that the rebuilding of the abbey was the definitive answer for today. At best, it was a sign of the need to rebuild the spirituality that Iona historically represents. But new birthings need to happen in our lives and relationships and communities again and again and again. Long after Iona Abbey was rebuilt in the twentieth century, Macleod uttered a prayer that has been with me almost daily over the last number of years. In it he imagines Christ faithfully going to the Temple in Jerusalem, which represented both a place of ancient faith and at the same time a place that needed new vision.

Macleod concludes the prayer by saying:

> Give us grace in our changing day
> to stand by the temple that is the present church,
> the noisome temple
> the sometime scandalised temple that is the present
> church,

listening sometime to what again seems mumbo
jumbo.
Make it our custom to go
till the new outline of your Body for our day
becomes visible in our midst.[1]

What is the "new outline" of Christ's body for
today? What is the new birthing of spirituality that is
trying to become visible within us and among us in our
world now?

Throughout this book, I have been pointing to a
way of seeing that has characterized the Celtic tradition
over the centuries. Particularly, it is a way of seeing
Christ that is distinct from most of our Western Christian
inheritance. It views Christ as coming from the heart of
creation rather than from beyond creation. And it cele-
brates him as reconnecting us to our true nature instead
of saving us from us our nature. Much of this seeing has
been influenced by the writings and perspective of John
the Beloved, who in the Celtic world represents a vision
of the sacred unity of life, all things coming forth from
the Heart of God's Being. John is symbolized by the eagle
in flight. It is as if he sees the oneness of creation and the
Light that is at the heart of all life from a great height.

A few years ago, during one of my writing weeks
in the high desert of New Mexico, I hiked into Box
Canyon, north of Abiquiu. It was mid-December, and

parts of the canyon were like a cold white underworld that received no direct daylight from the low winter sun. With the arroyo frozen, I was able to walk on the riverbed and at the same time hear the sound of flowing water beneath the ice. Here and there, great pine trees had fallen across the stream, so to proceed, I had to scramble over or under them. At one point, as I bent low beneath an old fallen pine, halfway under its massive trunk, I was met by something rushing in the opposite direction. In the silent winter canyon, it was a shock to be knocked off balance by a fast-moving creature. I had no idea what it was until, having leapt back in fright, I looked behind me and saw a great wingspan rising up from the ground. It was an eagle with a rabbit in her talons. She had been so intent on the catch that she had not noticed me, nor I her, but she had brushed against me under the fallen tree.

To have come that close to a mighty creature of the air was exhilarating. But my Heartbeat told me it was not just exhilaration. It was also fear. Physically, I had been startled by something I could never have imagined happening. Yet I knew it was more than simply a physical meeting. It was as if the spirit of the eagle had visited me, in such a way that I will always long for her company again. It was as if my soul had been brushed by her wings, in such a way that I will always long to know what she sees.

But over these few years, as I have thought about what it means to be brushed by an eagle, I have realized also that the urgency with which we must recover John the Eagle's perspective is not simply the height from which he sees life. It is also the intimacy with which he approaches the Heart of life with love. He is remembered as the one who leaned against Jesus at the Last Supper and heard the Heartbeat of God. He sees all things as one, from the greatest of heights as it were, but he also leans close to hear the strong but tender beat of God in all things.

In looking back on my walk into the canyon that winter afternoon, I see that I met the eagle not by climbing to higher ground but by leaning closer to the ground. It was as I bowed that I came in touch with a presence that surprised me. The new vision of reality that we are being invited to be part of, both individually and collectively, in which we are able to see the essential oneness of life and the interrelatedness of all things, is not a vision that will be ours by distancing ourselves from the earth or from the ground of the human soul. It is a vision that will further unfold within us and between us as together we move closer to the earth with reverence and allow ourselves to be surprised by the Presence that is within creation and within the human soul.

As I sit in the nunnery praying for new beginnings in my life and in the life of the world, I am aware that voices from many nations surround me—Japanese, German, American, French. I remember someone once asking me if I did not feel terribly cut off from the world on this remote Hebridean island. And I realized it is quite the opposite: rarely do I feel more in touch with the world than during my visits to this island—because the world comes to Iona, and often it comes with a wide-open soul, showing its pain and its longings.

Here in the nunnery, I hear in my own heart the stirrings of the human soul. This may be a place of ancient ruin, but it is a place also that shows the signs of a new birthing. It is a birthing that is happening in the hearts and lives of men and women throughout the world. This may be a place of crumbling stone, but it is a place also in which the inner foundations of a new spirituality are being laid. It is a spirituality that is emerging in the hopes and consciousness of communities everywhere. This may be a place in which it is impossible to define exactly what the relationship is between the many who pray here, but it is a place in which we are remembering that what we have lost affects us all. We may not know what the answers are, but we know that expressing our deepest longings for Presence and for connection is a key to the way forward.

In the nunnery, I hear that we are longing to live and pray in a closer relationship to the earth. In the nunnery, I hear that we are longing to find ways of doing this in relationship. And in the nunnery, I hear that we are longing for a greater consciousness of the One from whom we have come and who addresses us each by name. These are the longings I hear in my own heart. And I do not believe they belong simply to me. I believe they issue up from a place deep in the human soul. How are we to respond to them?

A number of years ago, as the little spirituality center of Casa del Sol in New Mexico was being conceived, I spoke with a native leader about the types of conversations we might have in a community of listening and dialogue. I asked, "What is it I am to bring to the table of humanity? What am I to bring to our relationship in this place?" He answered very simply and very challengingly: "Philip, bring your treasure—bring Christ." He then said, "Would you expect me, as a native leader, to bring something less than my greatest treasure? Would you be satisfied with something less? So I tell you, bring your treasure. Bring Christ."

I understand why those of us of liberal sensitivity in the Christian household have hesitated from bringing Christ to the table. In the past, he has been used to beat others over the head and to tell them they need to become "like us." So I understand the hesitation. I know why many of us have simply gone silent. But if we are to establish true relationships in the journey of the world today, as distinct cultures and religions and nations, we need to find ways of bringing our treasure to one another. And we need to do it now, with reverence and with costly self-giving, if there is to be healing. The treasure we carry is never simply our own. It belongs to the human soul. And in that sense, we are only giving it back. "Bring your treasure," he said. "Bring Christ."

As I sit in the nunnery, I am aware that this is my desire, to bring the treasure of our Christian household to the yearnings of the world today. And I am seeing that we can do it in new ways, in ways that listen reverently to the hunger of the human heart and in ways that will bring us closer to one another, as individuals and as distinct traditions, instead of into further separation and brokenness. This is a desire that issues up from deep in the soul. It is not a Christian desire or a Jewish or a Muslim desire. It is a holy human desire, and it will cost us much. But it is for the healing of creation.

Notes

Prelude

1 J. K. Elliot, ed., *The Apocryphal New Testament* (Oxford: Oxford University Press, 1999), p. 319.

2 Ibid.

Chapter One: The Memory of the Song

1 B. Layton, ed., *The Gnostic Scriptures* (London: SCM, 1987), p. 45.

2 Ibid., p. 48.

3 Ibid., p. 50.

4 J. S. Eriugena, *Periphyseon (The Division of Nature)*, trans. J. O'Meara (Montreal: Bellarmin, 1987), p. 592.

5 Ibid., p. 112.

6 P. Teilhard de Chardin, *The Prayer of the Universe*, trans. R. Hague. (London: Collins, 1977), p. 82.

7 Eriugena, *Periphyseon*, p. 131.

Chapter Two: A Forgotten Tune

1 *Book of Common Prayer* (Cambridge: Cambridge University Press, 1920), p. 227.

2 *Westminster Confession of Faith* (Glasgow: Free Presbyterian Publications, 1973), p. 40.

3 G. M. Hopkins, "That Nature Is a Heraclitean Fire," in *Poems and Prose of Gerard Manley Hopkins*, ed. W. H. Gardner (Harmondsworth, England: Penguin, 1970), p. 66.

Chapter Three: The Rhythm of the Earth

1 R. Grant, ed., *Irenaeus of Lyons* (London: Routledge, 1997), p. 150.

2 Ibid., p. 169.

3 Ibid., p. 173.

Chapter Four: Empty Notes

1 J. S. Eriugena, *The Voice of the Eagle*, trans. C. Bamford (New York: Lindisfarne Press, 1990), p. 37.

2 Eriugena, *Periphyseon*, p. 500.

Chapter Five: The Sound of Love

1 Julian of Norwich, *Revelation of Divine Love*, trans. E. Spearing (Harmondsworth, England: Penguin, 1998), p. 139.

2 Ibid., p. 123.

3 Ibid., p. 139.

4 Ibid., p. 129.

5 Ibid., p. 145.

6 Ibid., p. 58.

7 Julian of Norwich, *Showings*, trans. J. Walsh (Mahwah, N.J.: Paulist Press, 1978), p. 290.

8 Julian of Norwich, *Revelation of Divine Love*, p. 104.

9 Ibid., p. 146.

10 Ibid.

11 Ibid., p. 10.

12 Ibid., p. 103.

13 Ibid., p. 147.

14 Ibid., p. 107.

15 Ibid., p. 4.

16 Ibid., p. 80.

17 Ibid., p. 85.

18 Ibid., p. 170.

Chapter Six: Paying the Piper

1 Aelred of Rievaulx, *Spiritual Friendship*, trans. M. E. Laker (Kalamazoo, Mich.: Cistercian Publications, 1977), p. 76.

Chapter Seven: The Hymn of the Universe

1 R. Ferguson, ed., *Daily Readings with George Macleod* (London: Fount, 1991), p. 68.

2 P. Teilhard de Chardin, *The Heart of Matter*, trans. R. Hague. (London: Collins, 1978), p. 15.

3 U. King, *Spirit of Fire: The Life and Vision of Teilhard de Chardin* (New York: Orbis, 1996), p. 51.

4 Teilhard de Chardin, *Heart of Matter*, p. 17.

5 Ibid., p. 26.

6 P. Teilhard de Chardin, *Le Milieu Divin*, trans. R. Hague. (London: Collins, 1967), p. 78.

7 P. Teilhard de Chardin, "Cosmic Life," in *The Prayer of the Universe*, trans. R. Hague (London: Collins, 1977), p. 41.

8 Ibid., p. 89.

9 Ibid., p. 104.

10 King, *Spirit of Fire*, p. 102.

11 Teilhard de Chardin, *Le Milieu Divin*, p. 88.

12 Teilhard de Chardin, "Cosmic Life," p. 100.

13 Julian of Norwich, *Revelation of Divine Love*, p. 10.

Chapter Eight: Broken Cadences

1 Julian of Norwich, *Revelation of Divine Love*, p. 80.

2 Teilhard de Chardin, *Heart of Matter*, pp. 117–118.

3 King, *Spirit of Fire*, p. 94.

4 Ibid., p. 107.

5 Ibid., p. 141.

6 Ibid., p. 189.

7 Teilhard de Chardin, "Cosmic Life," p. 143.

8 Ibid.

9 King, *Spirit of Fire*, p. 151.

10 P. Teilhard de Chardin, *Christianity and Evolution*, trans. R. Hague (London: Collins, 1971), p. 128.

11 Teilhard de Chardin, *Le Milieu Divin*, p. 154.

12 King, *Spirit of Fire*, p. 148.

13 Teilhard de Chardin, *Christianity and Evolution*, p. 94.

14 Ibid., p. 95.

15 Teilhard de Chardin, *Le Milieu Divin*, p. 39.

16 Teilhard de Chardin, "Cosmic Life," p. 111.

17 King, *Spirit of Fire*, p. 124.

18 Ferguson, *Daily Readings*, p. 68.

19 Teilhard de Chardin, *Heart of Matter*, p. 53.

20 P. Teilhard de Chardin, *Comment Je Crois* (Paris: Editions du Seuil, 1969), p. 245. My translation.

Postlude

1 G. F. Macleod, *The Whole Earth Shall Cry Glory* (Glasgow, Scotland: Wild Goose, 1985), pp. 39–40.

The Author

J PHILIP NEWELL is a poet, scholar, and teacher. The former warden of Iona Abbey in the Western Isles of Scotland, he is now companion theologian for the American Spirituality Center of Casa del Sol at Ghost Ranch in the high desert of New Mexico. Casa del Sol is a Community of the Living Presence, seeking the oneness of the human soul and the healing of creation. Newell is internationally acclaimed for his work in the field of Celtic spirituality, including his much admired *Listening for the Heartbeat of God* and his poetic book of prayer, *Sounds of the Eternal*. He is a minister in the Church of Scotland and, in the ancient Celtic model, a wandering scholar, lecturing and leading retreats in various parts of the world. A Canadian by birth, Newell maintains his family base in Edinburgh, Scotland, where he undertook his doctoral research in Celtic Christianity. On both sides of the Atlantic, he plays a leading role in the rebirthing of spirituality for today. For more information, visit his Web site at www.jphilipnewell.com.